Maurice Merleau-Ponty
and His Critics

Garland Reference Library of the Humanities (vol. 51)

Maurice Merleau-Ponty and His Critics
An International Bibliography
(1942-1976)

*Preceded by a Bibliography
of
Merleau-Ponty's Writings*

**François Lapointe
Claire Lapointe**

Garland Publishing, Inc., New York & London

1976

Copyright © 1976

by François Lapointe

Claire Lapointe

All Rights Reserved

Library of Congress Cataloging in Publication Data

Lapointe, François.
  Maurice Merleau-Ponty and his critics.

  (Garland reference library of the humanities ; v. 51)
  1. Merleau-Ponty, Maurice, 1908-1961--Bibliography.
I. Lapointe, Claire, joint author. II. Title.
Z8570.45.L37 [B2430.M38] 016.194 75-42885
ISBN 0-8240-9949-4

Printed in the United States of America

CONTENTS

	Introduction	1
I.	Bibliography of Merleau-Ponty's Writings . . .	7
II.	Bibliography on Merleau-Ponty	31
	Books Devoted to Merleau-Ponty	33
	Doctoral Dissertations and Theses	45
	Studies of Individual Works by Merleau-Ponty .	53

    La Structure du Comportement (1942)   53

    Phénoménologie de la Perception (1945) . .   54

    Humanisme et Terreur (1947)   60

    Sens et Non-Sens (1948)   62

    Les Aventures de la Dialectique (1955) . .   63

    Signes (1960)   67

    L'Oeil et l'Esprit (1960)   68

    Le Visible et l'Invisible (1964)   69

    Eloge de la Philosophie (1953)   72

    LRS Relations de l'enfant avec Autrui . . .   74

    Resumes de cours au Collège de France 1952-1960 (1968)   74

    L'Union de l'ame et du corps chez Malebranche, Biran et Bergson (1968) . .   74

    La Prose du monde (1969)   75

    The Primacy and Perception and Other Essays (1964)   75

    Consciousness and the Acquisition of Language   76

    The Essential Writings of Merleau-Ponty . .   76

  General Discussion of the Works of Merleau-Ponty   77

CONTENTS

Items Arranged by Proper Names 88

Items Arranged by Subjects 103

INTRODUCTION

INTRODUCTION

In May 1976 we will commemorate the 15th anniversary of the sudden and premature death of Maurice Merleau-Ponty from a coronary thrombosis, a death which came as a grave shock to the whole of the philosophical and intellectual world. As Alphonse de Waelhens wrote at the time: "Il ne me souvient pas qu'une mort ait consterné davantage. Dans l'instant, nous avons perçu qu'une dimension de la vérité nous était retirée, qu'une expression du vrai, longuement attendue, ne serait jamais dite." The shock was not simply because one of the most important philosophers of our time had died. A deep and terrible loss was also felt because Merleau-Ponty had barely reached his prime, as philosophers go. It is certain that, had he lived, his philosophical contribution would have grown beyond its present size, impressive as that is.

It has not been sufficiently clear, as James M. Edie points out, that in *The Structure of Behavior* and the *Phenomenology of Perception* Merleau-Ponty is presenting a *thesis*, a program for phenomenological research, which would have to be developed, criticized, and tested over a considerable period of time and which should not be taken as prematurely established. The *Phenomenology of Perception* is clearly Merleau-Ponty's greatest single achievement and the book of his which is most likely to become a classic of twentieth-century philosophy. In this work it was Merleau-Ponty's intention to lay down a solid basis for phenomenological research which would take him forward from the phenomenology of perception to studies on imagination, language, culture, reason and on aesthetic, ethical, political, and even religious experience. That he was able to do no more than begin this work during his own lifetime is something that he was painfully aware of.

In the decade that followed his death, Merleau-Ponty's "gloire" suffered a partial eclipse in France, while his influence abroad increased markedly. It was a clear mark of the increasing influence of his thought in Anglo-American philosophy that within a few years of his death virtually all his writings were available in English.* It would not be accurate to say that there have not been any important studies of the work and thought of Merleau-Ponty in France during the last fifteen years. Among the contributions that immediately come

---

*As our bibliography of his writings indicates, by 1970 most of his works had been translated into German, Italian, Spanish and Portuguese.

to mind, we can mention Xavier Tilliette's book, *Merleau-Ponty ou la mesure de l'homme* (Seghers, 1970), François Heidsieck, *L'Ontologie de Merleau-Ponty* (Presses Universitaires de France, 1971), and many important articles by Claude Lefort. But this being granted, the fact remains, as Bernard Pingaud points out in the issue of *L'Arc* devoted to Merleau-Ponty, that "dix ans après la mort de Merleau-Ponty, un étrange silence règne dans les milieux intellectuels dit 'avancés': le nom de Merleau-Ponty n'est presque jamais cité par les penseurs à la mode." (p. 96). But there is clear indication that the situation is changing in France. A number of important books on Merleau-Ponty have recently been published in French by Ghyslain Charron, Gary B. Madison, Théodore F. Geraets, and more recently by Luce Fontaine-de Visscher.

It is quite natural that having just published a bibliography on Jean-Paul Sartre (Bowling Green, Ohio: Philosophy Documentation Center, 1975), we should turn to Merleau-Ponty.

Our bibliography attempts to show the wide range of critical response to Merleau-Ponty's writings. Since bibliography is an essential tool of philosophy as a kind of scholarship, we hope that this compilation of primacy and secondary materials will give Merleau-Ponty scholars some assistance.

The works listed here show that Merleau-Ponty's ideas are constantly being examined in new ways, in new contexts, and using new resources uncovered by investigations in a variety of fields. This bibliography provides proof that Merleau-Ponty's work is still found fresh and exciting by a new generation of scholars.

Bibliography always serves a utilitarian purpose. To compile as complete a collection of items as possible is one thing. To provide a useful arrangement of this collection is another thing. The major task of the bibliographer should be to bring order out of the chaos of alphabetic or chronological listing. The bibliography of secondary materials is divided into five major sections. The first one contains books devoted to Merleau-Ponty (or almost exclusively so), and the books are classified by language. Book reviews have been included when available. The second lists unpublished dissertations and theses, also indicating the entries, when available, in *Dissertation Abstracts International*. In the third section we have listed books and articles (as well as book reviews) devoted to a single work of Merleau-Ponty (arranged in a chronological order). In the fourth section, we have listed other items by proper names. This section

INTRODUCTION 5

includes material in which Merleau-Ponty is being compared or contrasted with major figures in philosophy or the social sciences. The remaining items are arranged by subject. Abundant cross-reference is used so that material can be located easily and quickly.

The bibliography is intended to be as complete as is technically feasible. Our purpose is to provide an accurate, reasonably complete and useful arrangement of materials for those interested in Merleau-Ponty. Although no bibliography can claim to be exhaustive, every attempt at completeness and accuracy has been made. All of the standard reference works known to us were consulted, and many periodicals and books were searched individually. Items through December 1975 are included.

Although we have made every effort to compile an accurate, up-to-date, and reasonably complete bibliography, we are fully aware of the provisional nature of our work and feel no obligation to apologize for this. As is well known to bibliographers, publication constitutes a stage in the movement toward completeness, a more or less 'complete' starting point for further work. Our hope is that eventually we can come closer to our ideal of completeness in a supplementary volume, or a second edition, which will continue this one beyond 1975, and which will include earlier items we were regrettably unable to include (for one reason or another), as well as corrections of possible errors.

It is impossible in an extensive bibliography to remove all errors and make good all gaps of information. Since we intend to issue a supplementary volume, or a revised edition, we urgently solicit the help of those who use this bibliography. Please send us corrections, leads, and information. We would be pleased to hear from students of Merleau-Ponty, especially those in Scandinavia as well as Central and East Europe and Latin America, who are frustrated by our omissions.

François and Claire Lapointe
Tuskegee Institute, Alabama   36088
U.S.A.

PART ONE

BIBLIOGRAPHY OF MERLEAU-PONTY'S WRITINGS

1935

1. "Christianisme et ressentiment." *La Vie Intellectuelle*, 7e année, nouvelle série, T. XXXVI, 10 juin 1935, pp. 278-306. [A review of Max Scheler's book *Ressentiment*.] English trans, "Christianity and Ressentiment." (Trans. by C. G. Wening.) *Review of Existential Psychology and Psychiatry*, vol. IX, no. 1, 1968, pp. 1-22.

1936

2. "Etre et avoir." *La Vie Intellectuelle*, 8e année, nouvelle série, T. XLV, 10 octobre 1936, pp. 98-106. [A review of Gabriel Marcel's book, *Etre et avoir*. Paris: Aubier, 1935.]

3. "Jean-Paul Sartre. *L'Imagination*." *Journal de Psychologie Normale et Pathologique*, 33e année, no. 9-10, 1936, Novembre-décembre 1936, pp. 756-761. [A review of Sartre's book, *L'Imagination*. Paris: Librairie Félix Alcan, 1936.]

4. "Quelques aspects et quelques développements de la psychologie de la forme." Aron Gurwitsch (with the collaboration of Merleau-Ponty). *Journal de Psychologie Normale et Pathologique*, 33e année, 1936.

1939

5. "L'agrégation de philosophie." Intervention à la Société française de Philosophie, séance du 7 mai, 1938. *Bulletin de la Société Française de Philosophie*, 38e année, no. 4, juillet-août 1938, pp. 130-133.

1942

6. *La Structure du Comportement*. Paris: Presses Universitaires de France, 1942. VIII-395pp. 2e ed. (1949) et suivantes, précédé de "Une philosophie de l'ambiguïté" par A. De Waelhens, XV-248pp. English trans. by Alden L. Fisher, *The Structure of Behavior*. Boston. Beacon Press, 1963- London: Methuen & Co., 1965. Spanish trans. by E. Alonso, *La Estructura del Comportamiento*. Buenos Aires: Librería Hachette, 1957.

10   MERLEAU-PONTY'S WRITINGS

Italian trans. by G. D. Neri, *La Struttura del Comportamento*. Milano: Bompiani, 1963.

1943

7   "*Les Mouches* par J.-P. Sartre." *Confluences*, 3e année, no. 25, septembre-octobre 1943, pp. 514-516. [A review of Sartre's play.]

1945

8   *Phénoménologie de la Perception*. Paris: Gallimard, 1945, XVI-531pp.
English trans. by Colin Smith. *Phenomenology of Perception*. New York: Humanities Press, 1962- London: Routledge and Kegan Paul, 1962.
English trans. of the "Preface" by John F. Bannan, "What is Phenomenology?" *Cross Currents*, Vol. VI, 1955, pp. 56-70.
"What is Phenomenology?" in Alden L. Fisher, *The Essential Writings of Merleau-Ponty*, pp. 27-43. New York: Harcourt, Brace and World Pub., 1970.
German trans. by R. Boehm, *Phänemenologie der Wahrnehmung*. Berlin: Walter de Gruyter, 1966.
Spanish trans. by E. Uranga, *Fenomenología de la Percepción*. México: Fondo de Cultura Económica, 1957.
Italian trans. by A. Bonomi, *Fenomenologia della percezione*. Il Saggiatore, 1965.
Portuguese trans. by Reginaldo di Piero, *Fenomenologia da percepção*. Rio de Janeiro: Liv. Freitas Bastos, 1971.

9   "La guerre a eu lieu." dated June 1945. *Les Temps Modernes*, Ière année, no. 1, octobre 1945, pp. 48-66.
Reprinted in *Sens et Non-sens*. Paris: Nagel, 1948, pp. 245-269.
"The War Has Taken Place," pp. 139-152 in *Sense and Non-sense*, translated by Hubert L. Dreyfus and Patricia Allen Dreyfus, Evanston, Illinois: North western University Press, 1964.

10   "La Querelle de l'Existentialisme." *Les Temps Modernes*, Ière année, no. 2, novembre 1945, pp. 344-356.
Reprinted in *Sens et Non-sens*, pp. 123-143.-
Sense and Non-sense, "The Battle Over Existentialism," pp. 71-82.

11 "Roman et Métaphysique." *Cahiers du Sud*, T. XXII, no. 270, mars-avril 1945, pp. 194-207.
Reprinted in *Sens et Non-sens*, "Le Roman et la Métaphysique," pp. 45-71.
"Metaphysics and the Novel," in *Sense and Non-sense*, pp. 26-40.

12 "Le Doute de Cézanne." *Fontaine*, 4e année, T. VIII, no. 47, décembre 1945, pp. 80-100. Reprinted in *Sens et Non-sens*, pp. 15-44.
"Cézanne's Doubt," in *Sense and Non-sense*, pp. 9-25. Also in *The Partisan Review*, vol. XIII, no. 4, Sept.-October 1946, pp. 464-478. Also in Alden Fisher's *The Essential Writings of Merleau-Ponty*, pp. 233-251.

1946

13 "Pour la Vérité." (dated Novembre 1945). *Les Temps Modernes*, 1ère année, no. 4, janvier 1945, pp. 577-600.
Reprinted in *Sens et non-sens*, pp. 271-304.
"For the Sake of Truth," in *Sense and Non-sense*, pp. 153-171.

14 "Foi et bonne foi." *Les Temps Modernes*, 1ère année, no. 5, février 1946, pp. 769-782.
Reprinted in *Sens et non-sens*, pp. 305-324.
"Faith and Good Faith," in *Sense and Non-sense*, pp. 172-181. Also in Fisher, *The Essential Writings of Merleau-Ponty*, pp. 353-363.

15 "Autour du Marxisme." *Fontaine*, 5e année, no. 48-49, janvier-février 1946, pp. 309-331. [dated about 1945.]
Reprinted in *Sens et Non-sens*, pp. 173-220.
"Concerning Marxism," pp. 99-124 in *Sense and Non-sense*.

16 "Le Culte du Héros." *Action*, Hebdomadaire de la Libération française, no. 74, 1 février 1946, pp. 12-13.
Reprinted under the title, "Le Héros, l'Homme," pp. 323-331 in *Sens et Non-sens*.
"Man, the Hero," pp. 182-187 in *Sense and Non-sense*.

17 "L'Existentialisme chez Hegel." *Les Temps Modernes*, 1ère année, no. 7, avril 1946, pp. 1311-1319. [à propos d'une Conféerence donnée par Jean Hyppolite le 16 février 1945 à l'Institut des Hautes Etudes Germaniques.]
Reprinted in *Sens et Non-sens*, pp. 109-122. [Mistakenly dated February 1947.]

12   MERLEAU-PONTY'S WRITINGS

"Hegel's Existentialism," pp. 63-70 in *Sense and Non-sense*.

18   "Marxisme et Philosophie." *Revue Internationale*, 1ère année, 1945-1946, no. 6, juin-juillet 1946, pp. 518-526.
Reprinted in *Sens et Non-sens*, pp. 221-241.
"Marxism and Philosophy," [abridged trans.], *Politics*, IV, 1947, pp. 173-175.
"Marxism and Philosophy," in *Sense and Non-sense*, pp. 125-136.

19   "Faut-il brûler Kaffka?" *Action*, Hebdomadaire de la Libération française, no. 97, 12 juillet 1946, pp. 14-15.

20   "Le Yogi et le Prolétaire," (I), [First title under which appeared the articles subsequently published in book form, under the title *Humanisme et Terreur* (1947)].
Les Temps Modernes, 2e année, 1946-47, no. 13, octobre 1946, pp. 1-29.
Reprinted in *Humanisme et Terreur*, pp. 3-48.

21   "Le Yogi et le Prolétaire" (II). *Les Temps Modernes*, 2e année, 1946-47, no. 14, novembre 1946, pp. 253-287.
Reprinted in *Humanisme et Terreur*, pp. 48-75, 100-105, 111-141.

1947

22   "Le Yogi et le Prolétaire," (III). *Les Temps Modernes*, 2e année, 1946-47, no. 16, janvier 1947, pp. 676-711.
Reprinted in *Humanisme et Terreur*, pp. 141-206.
English trans. of pp. 161-191, by Nancy Metzel and John Flodstrom, under the title, "The Yogi and the Proletarian," pp. 211-228, in *The Primacy of Perception* and other essays on phenomenological psychology, the philosophy of art, history and politics. Edited, with an Introduction by James M. Edie. Evanston, Illinois: Northeastern University Press, 1964.

23   *L'Esprit européen*, Recontres internationales de Genève, 1946. Neuchâtel: Les Editions de la Baconnière, 1947; intervention de Merleau-Ponty, pp. 74-77, 133, 252-256.

24 "Le primat de la perception et ses conséquences philosophiques," *Bulletin de la Société française de Philosophie*, 41e année, 1947, (séance du 23 novembre, 1946), pp. 119-135, discussion pp. 135-153. English trans. by James M. Edie in *The Primacy of Perception and Other Essays*, edited, with an Introduction by James M. Edie. Evanston, Illinois: Northwestern University Press, 1964, pp. 12, 42. Also in Alden Fisher, *The Essential Writings of Merleau-Ponty*, pp. 47-63.

25 "Indochine S.O.S." *Les Temps Modernes*, 2e année, 1946-47, no. 18, mars 1947, pp. 1039-1052. Reprinted in *Signes*, "Sur L'Indochine, pp. 402-407 [pp. 1039-1044 de l'article original]. "On Indo-China," English trans. by Richard C. McLeary in *Signs*, pp. 323-327. Evanston, Illinois: Northwestern University Press, 1964.

26 "Pour les Rencontres Internationales." *Les Temps Modernes*, 2e année, 1946-47, no. 19, avril 1947, pp. 1340-1344.

27 "Apprendre à lire," *Les Temps Modernes*, 3e année, 1947-48, no. 22, juillet 1947, pp. 1-27. Reprinted in the "Préface" to *Humanisme et Terreur*, IX-XLIII.

28 "Le Métaphysique dans l'Homme." *Revue de Métaphysique et de Morale*, 52e année, juillet-octobre 1947, no. 3-4, pp. 290-307. Reprinted in *Sens et Non-sens*, pp. 145-172. "The Metaphysical in Man," in *Sense and Non-sense*, pp. 83-98.

29 "Le Cinéma et la nouvelle Psychologie" [conférence given March 13, 1945, at l'Institut des Hautes Etudes Cinématographiques]. *Les Temps Modernes*, 3e année, 1947-48, no. 26, novembre 1947, pp. 930-943. Reprinted in *Sens et Non-sens*, pp. 85-106. "The Film and the New Psychology," in *Sense and Non-sense*, pp. 48-59. "Das Kino und die neue Psychologie." *Filmkritik*, II, 1969, pp. 695-702 (trans. by F. Grafe).

30 "En un combat douteux." [signed T.M.] *Les Temps Modernes*, 3e année, 1947-48, no. 27, décembre 1947, pp. 961-964.

31 "Lecture de Montaigne." *Les Temps Modernes*, 3e année, 1947-48, no. 27, 1947-48, no. 27, décembre 1947, pp. 1044-1060. Reprinted in *Signes*, pp. 250-266. "Reading Montaigne," pp. 198-210 in *Signs*.

MERLEAU-PONTY'S WRITINGS

32 "Les Cahiers de la Pléiade." *Les Temps Modernes*, 3e année, 1947-48, no. 27, décembre 1947, pp. 1151-1152.

33 "Jean-Paul Sartre, ou un auteur scandaleux." *Le Figaro Littéraire*, 2e année, no. 85, 6 décembre 1947, pp. 1, 3.
Reprinted with the title "Un auteur scandaleux," in *Sens et Non-sens*, pp. 73-84.
"A Scandalous Author," in *Sense and Non-sense*, pp. 41-47.

34 *Humanisme et Terreur. Essai sur le problème communiste.* Paris: Gallimard, 1947, XLIII-206pp.
English trans. by John O'Neill, *Humanism and Terror, an Essay on the Communist Problem.* Boston: Beacon Press, 1969, XLVII-189pp.
German trans. by E. Moldenhauer, *Humanismus und Terror I & II.* Frankfurt am Main: Suhrkamp, 1966.
Spanish trans, *Humanismo y Terror.* Buenos Aires: Ediciones Leviatán, 1956.
Italian trans. by A. Bonomi & F. Madonia, *Umanesimo e terrore. Le Avventure della dialettica.* Milano: Sugar, 1965.

35 *Academic Year 1947-48*, Université de Lyon. [Lectures on general psychology and aesthetic; lectures on history of philosophy: La liberté chez Leibniz (Unpublished)].

1948

36 *Sens et Non-sens.* Paris: Nagel, 1948, 380 pp. Subsequent editions 331 pp. [Collection of the following articles and preceded by Preface]: Contains: Part I ARTS: 1-Cézanne's Doubt (12); 2-Metaphysics and the Novel (11); 3-A Scandalous Author (33); 4-The Film and the New Psychology (29). Part II: IDEAS: 5-Hegel's Existentialism (17); 6-The Battle over Existentialism (10); 7-The Metaphysical in Man (28); 8-Concerning Marxism (15); 9-Marxism and Philosophy (18). Part III: POLITICS: 10-The War Has Taken Place (9); 11-For the Sake of Truth (13); 12-Faith and Good Faith (14); 13-Man, the Hero (16).
English trans. by Hubert L. Dreyfus and Patricia Allen Dreyfus, *Sense and Non-sense.* Evanston, Illinois: Northwestern University Press, 1964.
Italian trans. by P. Caruso, *Senso e Non-senso.* Milano: Il Saggiatore, 1962.
Spanish trans., *Existencialismo y marxismo.* Buenos Aires: Deucalion, 1957. [Trans. of the 2nd part of *Sens et Non-sens*].

37	"Le Manifeste communiste a cent ans." *Le Figaro Littéraire*, 3 avril 1948, pp. 6-8.
38	"Complicité objective." *Les Temps Modernes*, 4e année, 1948-49, no. 34, juillet 1948, pp. 1-11. [Editorial signed T.M.]
39	"Communisme et anticommunisme." *Les Temps Modernes*, 4e année, 1948-49, no. 34, juillet 1948, pp. 175-188. Reprinted in *Signes* under the title of "La Politique paranoïaque," pp. 309-328. "Paranoid Politics," pp. 247-260 in *Signs*.
40	Dumas, J.-L. "Les Conférences." *La Nef*, 5e année, no. 45, août 1948, pp. 150-151. [A summary by Dumas of an unpublished lecture given by Merleau-Ponty entitled "L'Homme et l'objet."]
41	Academic Year 1948-49, Université de Lyon. Lectures on general psychology: Langage et communication; Lectures on history of philosophy: Ame et corps chez Malebranche, Maine de Biran, Bergson (unpublished).

1949

42	"Machiavélisme et Humanisme," [communication au Congrès 'Umanesimo e scienza politica' September 1949, Rome-Florence.] Reprinted in *Les Temps Modernes*, 5e année, 1949-50, no. 48, octobre 1949, pp. 577-593. Also in *Atti del Congresso Internazionale di Studi Umanistici*. Roma-Firenze, sept. 1949, a cura di Enrico Castelli. Milano: Marzorati, 1951, pp. 297-308. Reprinted in *Signes*, under the title of "Note sur Machiavel," pp. 267-283. "A Note on Machiavelli," pp. 211-223 in *Signs*.
43	"Lukács et l'autocritique." *Les Temps Modernes*, 5e année, 1949-50, no. 50, décembre 1949, pp. 1119-1121. [Commentaire sur un article de François Erval consacré à Georg Lukács]. Reprinted in *Signes*, under the title of "Marxisme et superstition," pp. 328-330. "Marxism and Superstition," in *Signs*, pp. 261-262.
44	"Humanisme surréaliste et humanisme existentialiste." [Lecture delivered at the Collège Philosophique, 1949, (unpublished).]

MERLEAU-PONTY'S WRITINGS

45 "Les Jours de notre vie." *Les Temps Modernes*, 5e année, 1949-50, no. 51, janvier 1950, pp. 1153-1168 [in collaboration with Jean-Paul Sartre]. Reprinted in *Signes* under the title of "L'U.R.S.S. et les camps," pp. 330-343.
"The U.S.S.R. and the Camps," pp. 263-273 in *Signs*.

46 "Mort d'Emmanuel Mounier." *Les Temps Modernes*, 5e année, 1949-50, no. 54, avril 1950, pp. 1906.

47 "Réponse à C. L.R. James" [signed T.M.] *Les Temps Modernes*, 5e année, 1949-50, no. 56, juin 1950, pp. 2292-2294.

48 "L'adversaire est complice." [signed T.M.] *Les Temps Modernes*, 6e année, 1950-51, no. 57, juillet 1950, pp. 1-11.

49 Academic Year 1950-51, Sorbonne. Lectures on general psychology: "Les Sciences de l'homme et la phénoménologie," Première partie. Paris: Centre de Documentation Universitaire, 1950-51. Réédité en 1961.
English trans. by John Wild, "Phenomenology and the Sciences of Man," pp. 43-95 in *The Primacy of Perception and Other Essays*, edited by James Edie, 1964.

1951

50 *Les Relations avec autrui chez l'enfant*, (cours de 1950-51). Les Cours de Sorbonne, Paris: Centre de Documentation universitaire, 60pp.
English trans. by William Cobb, "The Child's Relations with Others," pp. 96-155 in James Edie, ed., *The Primacy of Perception and Other Essays*, 1964. Italian trans. by G. Goela, *Il Bambino e gli altri*. Int. di Paolo Fileasi. (Collana diretta da G. Goela & R. Mazzetti, 6). Roma: A. Armando, 1968.

51 "Le Philosophe et la sociologie." *Cahiers Internationaux de Sociologie*, 6e année, juillet 1951, pp. 50-69.
Reprinted in *Signes*, pp. 123-142.
"The Philosopher and Sociology," pp. 98-113 in *Signes*. Also English trans. by Harvey G. Rabbin in *Philosophy of the Social Sciences*, ed. by Maurice Natanson. New York: Random House, 1963, pp. 487-505. Also in Alden Fisher, *The Essential Writings of Merleau-Ponty*, pp. 64-80.

52 "Introduction" [signed T.M.] to "Human Engineering," par Michel Crozier. *Les Temps Modernes*, 7e année, 1951-52, no. 69, juillet 1951, pp. 44-48.

1952

53 "L'homme et l'advertité." [conférence du 10 septembre 1951], in *La Connaissance de l'homme au XXe siècle*. Rencontres internationales de Genève, 1951. Neuchâtel: Les Editions de la Baconnière, 1952, conférence pp. 51-75, interventions pp. 182-183, 215-252, 286-287, 293-294.
Reprinted in *Signes*, pp. 284-308. [Without the discussions.]
"Man and Adversity," pp. 224-243 in *Signs*. Also in Fisher, *The Essential Writings of Merleau-Ponty*, pp. 91-111.
German trans., "Der Mensch und die Widerständigkeit des Daseins." *Merkur*, VI, 1952, pp. 801-821.
Spanish trans. by M. Riaza, "El hombre y la adversidad. Segunda discussion sobre la conferencia de Merleau-Ponty, en *Hombre y Cultura en el siglo XX*. Madrid: Guadarrama, 1957, pp. 113-142, pp. 172-206.

54 "Sur la phénoménologie du langage." *Problèmes actuels de la Phénoménologie*, Actes du premier Colloque international de phénoménologie. Bruxelles, avril 1951. Paris: Desclée de Brouwer, 1952, pp. 89-109.
Reprinted in *Signes*, pp. 105-122.
"On the Phenomenology of Language," pp. 84-97 in *Signs*. Also in Fisher, *The Essential Writings of Merleau-Ponty*, pp. 214-229.

55 *Les Sciences de l'homme et la phénoménologie* (cours de 1951-52). Les Cours de Sorbonne. Paris: Centre de Documentation Universitaire, 56pp. [First part of a two-year course. A summary of the complete course is to be found in *Maurice Merleau-Ponty à la Sorbonne* (1964).]

56 "Le langage indirect et les voix du silence, (I)." *Les Temps Modernes*, 7e année, 1951-52, no. 80, juin 1952, pp. 2113-2144.
Reprinted in *Signes*, pp. 49-81.

57 "Le langage indirect et les voix du silence (II)," *Les Temps Modernes*, 8e année, 1952-53, no. 81, juillet 1952, pp. 70-94.
Reprinted in *Signes*, pp. 81-104.
"Indirect Language and the Voices of Silence," pp. 39-83 in *Signs*.

18 MERLEAU-PONTY'S WRITINGS

"Das mittelbare Sprechen und die Stimmen des Schweigens," in *Das Auge und der Geist. Philosophische Essays.* (Trans. by H. W. Arnd). Hamburg: Rowohlt, 1967.

1953

58 *Eloge de la philosophie.* Leçon Inaugurale au Collège de France, le jeudi 15 janvier 1953. Paris: Gallimard. 91pp.
English trans. by James M. Edie and John Wild, *In Praise of Philosophy.* Evanston, Illinois: Northwestern University Press, 1963. Also in Fisher, *The Essential Writings of Merleau-Ponty,* pp. 17-26 (abridged).
German trans. by A. Metraux, *Lob der Philosophie,* in *Vorlesungen, I.* Berlin, New York: de Gruyter, 1973.
German trans. by H. W. Arnd, "Lob der Philosophie," in *Das Auge und der Geist. Philosophische Essays.* Hamburg: Rowohlt, 1967.
Spanish trans. by A. Letellier, *Elogio de la filosofía.* Buenos Aires: Ed. Galatea-Nueva Visión, 1957.
Italian trans. by E. Paci, *Elogio della filosofia.* Torino: G. B. Paravia, 1958.
Portuguese trans. by A. Braz Teixeira, *Elogie de filosofia.* Lisboa: Guimaraes Editores, 1962.

59 "Le monde sensible et le monde de l'expression," (cours du jeudi). *Annuaire du Collège de France.* Paris: Imprimerie Nationale, pp. 145-150.

60 "Recherches sur l'usage littéraire du langage" (cours du lundi). *Annuaire du Collège de France.* Paris: Imprimerie Nationale, pp. 150-155.
Both summaries of Merleau-Ponty's courses at the Collège de France were published in book form under the title, *Résumés de cours, Collège de France 1952-1960.* Paris: Gallimard, 1968. pp. 33-42, 43-56.
English trans. by John O'Neill. *Themes from the Lectures at the Collège de France 1952-1960.* "The Sensible World and the Value of Expression," pp. 3-11, "Studies in the Literary Use of Language," pp. 12-18.
Spanish trans. by H. Acevedo, *Filosofía y Lenguaje: resúmenes de los cursos del Collège de France.* Buenos Aires: Proteo, 1969.

1954

61 "Où sont les nouveaux maîtres?" *L'Express*, no. 71, 2 octobre 1954, p. 4.

62 "Le Philosophe est-il un fonctionnaire?" *L'Express*, no. 72, 9 octobre 1954, p. 3.

63 "Le libertin est-il un philosophe?" *L'Express*, no. 73, 16 octobre 1954, pp. 3-4.
Reprinted in *Signes*, "Sur l'érotisme," pp. 385-387.
"On Eroticism," in *Signs*, pp. 309-310.

64 "La France va-t-elle se renouveller?" *L'Express*, no. 74, 23 octobre 1954, pp. 3-4.

65 "Les femmes sont-elles des hommes?" *L'Express*, no. 76, 6 novembre 1954, p. 4.

66 "Les peuples se fâchent-ils?" *L'Express*, no. 80, 4 décembre 1954, pp. 3-4.

67 "Le goût pour les faits divers est-il malsain?" *L'Express*, no. 82, 18 décembre 1954, pp. 3-4.
Reprinted in *Signes* with the title "Sur les faits divers," pp. 388-391.
"On News Items," in *Signs*, pp. 311-313.

68 "Le problème de la parole" (cours du jeudi)

69 "Matériaux pour une théorie de l'histoire," (cours du lundi). *Annuaire du Collège de France*, pp. 175-179, and 180-187.
Reprinted in *Résumés de cours*, pp. 33-42, 43-56.
"The Problem of Speech," and "Materials for a Theory of History," pp. 19-26, and 27-38 in *Themes from the Lectures at the Collège de France*.

1955

70 "D'abord comprendre les communistes." *L'Express*, no. 85, 8 janvier 1955, pp. 8-9.

71 "A quoi sert l'objectivité?" *L'Express*, no. 88, 29 janvier 1955, p. 4.

72 "Comment répondre à Oppenheimer?" *L'Express*. no. 91, 19 février 1955, p. 3.

20   MERLEAU-PONTY'S WRITINGS

73 "Claudel était-il un génie?" *L'Express*, no. 93, 5 mars 1955, pp. 3-4.
Reprinted in *Signes*, "Sur Claudel," pp. 391-397.
"On Claudel," in *Signs*, pp. 314-318.

74 "M. Poujade a-t-il une petite cervelle?" *L'Express*, no. 95, 19 mars, 1955, p. 3.

75 "Le marxisme est-il mort à Yalta?" *L'Express*, no. 98, 9 avril 1955, pp. 3-4.
Reprinted in *Signes*, "Les papiers de Yalta," pp. 343-348.
"The Yalta Papers," pp. 274-277 in *Signs*.

76 "Sartre est un ultra-bolchéviste'...déclare Merleau-Ponty." *Le Figaro Littéraire*, 7 mai 1955, p. 1.

77 "Einstein et la crise de la raison." *L'Express*, no. 103, 14 mai 1955, p. 13.
Reprinted in *Signes*, pp. 242-249.
"Einstein and the Crisis of Reason," pp. 192-197 in *Signs*.

78 "Où va l'anti-communisme?" *L'Express*, no. 109, 25 juin 1955, p. 12.

79 "La majorité a-t-elle raison?" *L'Express*, no. 111, 9 juillet 1955, p. 12.
Reprinted in *Signes*, "Sur l'abstention," pp. 397-401.
"On Abstaining," in *Signs*, pp. 319-323.

80 "L'avenir de la révolution." *L'Express*, no. 118, 27 août 1955, pp. 7-10.
Reprinted in *Signes*, pp. 348-366.
"The Future of the Revolution," in *Signs*, pp. 278-292.

81 "L'institution dans l'histoire personnelle et publique," (cours du jeudi).

82 "Le problème de la passivité: le sommeil, l'inconscient, la mémoire," (cours du lundi).
Annuaire du Collège de France, pp. 157-160, 161-164.
Reprinted in *Résumés de Cours*, pp. 59-65, 60-73.
"Institutions in Personal and Public History," pp. 39-49, "The Problem of Passivity: Sleep, the Unconscious, Memory," pp. 46-52 in *Themes from the Collège de France, 1952-1960*.

83   *Les Aventures de la dialectique.* Paris: Gallimard, 1955. 313pp.
      English trans. by Joseph Bien, *Adventures of the dialectic.* Evanston, Illinois: Northwestern University Press, 1973, xxix-237pp.
      German trans. by Alfred Schmidt und Herbert Schmidt, *Die Abenteuer der Dialektik.* Frankfurt am Main: Suhrkamp, 1968.
      Spanish trans. by L. Rozitchner, *Las aventuras de la dialéctica.* Buenos Aires: Ediciones Leviatán, 1957.
      Italian trans. by A, Bonomi e F. Madonia, *Le Avventure della dialettica.* Milano: Sugar, 1965.

1956

84   "La philosophie dialectique," (cours du jeudi),

85   "Textes et commentaires sur la dialectique," (cours du lundi). *Annuaire du Collège de France,* 56e année, 1956-57, (cours de 1955-56), pp. 175-179, 179-180.
      Reprinted in *Résumés de cours,* pp. 77-84, 85-87.

86   *Les Philosophes célèbres.* Paris: Mazenod, 1956. [Work published under the direction of Merleau-Ponty, who wrote introductions for each of the major sections in this book, all but two of which are reprinted in *Signes.*] Contains:
      "Avant-Propos," pp. 7-12. Reprinted in *Signes,*
      "La philosophie et le 'dehors'," pp. 158-167.
      "Philosophy and the 'Outside'," in *Signs,* pp. 126-133.
      "-L'Orient et la philosophie," pp. 14-18. Reprinted in *Signes,* pp. 167-170. "The Orient and Philosophy," in *Signs,* pp. 133-140.
      "Les fondateurs," pp. 44-45.
      "Christianisme et philosophie," pp. 104-109. Reprinted in *Signes,* pp. 176-185. "Christianity and Philosophy," in *Signs,* pp. 140-146.
      "Le grand rationalisme," pp. 134-137. Reprinted in *Signes,* pp. 185-191. "Major Rationalism," in *Signs,* pp. 147-152.
      "Ia découverte de la subjectivité," pp. 186-187. Reprinted in *Signes,* pp. 191-194. "The Discovery of Subjectivity," in *Signs,* pp. 152-154.
      "La découverte de l'histoire," pp. 250-251, "Existence et dialectique," pp. 288-291. Reprinted in *Signes,* pp. 194-200.
      "Existence and Dialectic," in *Signs,* pp. 154-158.

22   MERLEAU-PONTY'S WRITINGS

87   "Premier dialogue Est-Ouest à Venise." *L'Express*, no. 278, 19 octobre 1956, pp. 21-24.

88   "Discordia Concors, Rencontre Est-Ouest à Venise."
Comprendre, Revue de politique de la culture, (Société Européenne de Culture près de la Biennale Venise), no. 16, septembre 1956, pp. 201-301. [Public discussions held in nine sittings, March 26-31, 1956. A condensed account with excerpts can be found in "Entre Merleau-Ponty, Sartre, Silone et les écrivains soviétiques: premier dialogue est-ouest à Venise," in *L'Express*, 19 octobre 1956, pp. 21-24.] Interventions by Merleau-Ponty, pp. 210-213, 214, 216, 217, 226, 227-228, 229, 237, 252-253, 265, 266, 267, 268, 271, 275-276, 278, 284, 285, 286, 287, 295, 296, 297.

89   "Réforme ou maladie sénile du communisme?" *L'Express*, no. 283, 23 novembre 1956, pp. 13-17.
Reprinted in *Signes*, "Sur la déstalinisation," pp. 366-385.
"On De-Stalinization," pp. 293-308 in *Signs*.

90   "Sur les rapports entre la mythologie et le rituel."
Bulletin de la Société française de Philosophie 50e année, juillet-septembre 1956. [Session of May 26, 1956 in which, among others, Lacan, Goldmann, Jean Wahl and Merleau-Ponty took part. Paper read by Serge Leclaire.]

1957

91   "La psychanalyse et son enseignement." *Bulletin de la Société française de Philosophie*, 51e année, avril-juin 1956, pp. 65-104. [A discussion in which Merleau-Ponty makes a comment on pp. 98-99. Paper read by J. Lacan.]

92   "Le concept de Nature (I) (cours du lundi et du jeudi). *Annuaire du Collège de France*, 57e année, cours de 1957-58, pp. 201-217.
Reprinted in *Résumés de cours*, pp. 91-121.
"The Concept of Nature, I." in *Themes from the Collège de France*, pp. 62-87.

1958

93   "Le concept de nature (suite). L'animalité, le corps humain, passage à la culture" (cours du mercredi et du jeudi). *Annuaire du Collège de France*, 58e année, (cours de 1958-59), pp. 312-319.

Reprinted in *Résumés de cours*, pp. 125-137.
"The Concept of Nature II: Animality, the Human Body, Transition to Culture," in *Themes from the Collège de France*, pp. 88-98.

94 "Du moindre mal à l'union sacrée." *Le Monde*, 5 juin 1958, p. 4 (Libres opinions).
Reprinted in *Signes*, "Sur le 13 mai 1958," pp. 418-423.
"On May 13, 1958," in *Signs*, pp. 337-340.

95 "La démocratie peut-elle renaître en France?" [interview]. *L'Express*, no. 368, 3 juillet 1958, pp. 15-17.
Reprinted in *Signes*, "Demain...", pp. 423-435.
"Tomorrow," in *Signs*, pp. 341-350.

96 "La France en Afrique," [interview]. *L'Express*, no. 375, 21 aout 1958, pp. 12-13.
Reprinted in *Signes*, "Sur Madagascar," pp. 408-418.
"On Madagascar," in *Signs*, pp. 328-336.

97 "Roger Martin du Gard." *L'Express*, no. 376, 28 août 1958.

1959

98 Cours sans titre: Réflexions générales sur le sens de l'ontologie de la nature et sur la possibilité de la philosophie d'aujourd'hui. *Annuaire du Collège de France*, 59e année, 1959-60, pp. 229-237.
Reprinted in *Résumés de cours*, pp. 141-156.
"Philosophy as Interrogation," in *Themes from the Collège de France*, pp. 99-112.

99 "Commentaire sur l'idée de la phénoménologie." *Husserl*, Cahiers de Royaumont (Philosophie III). Paris: Editions de Minuit, 1959. [Intervention by Merleau-Ponty, pp. 157-159.]

100 "Le Philosophe et son ombre." *Edmund Husserl, 1859-1959*. Recueil commémoratif publié à l'occasion du centenaire de la naissance du philosophe. Edited by H. L. Van Breda & J. Taminiaux. The Hague: Martinus Nijhoff, 1959. (Phaenomenologica 4), pp. 195-220.
Reprinted in *Signes*, pp. 201-228.
"The Philosopher and his Shadow," in *Signs*, pp. 159-181.

MERLEAU-PONTY'S WRITINGS

101   "De Mauss à Claude Lévi-Strauss." *La Nouvelle Revue Française*, 7e année, T. 14, no. 82, 1 octobre, 1959, pp. 615-631.
Reprinted in *Signes*, pp. 143-157.
"From Mauss to Claude Lévi-Strauss," in *Signs*, pp. 114-125.

102   "L'avenir du socialisme." [Débat présidé par Merleau-Ponty.] *Cahiers de la République*, No. XXLL, novembre-décembre 1959, pp. 27, 31-32, 35, 42.

1960

103   Discours prononcé le 19 mai 1959 lors de la séance d'hommage à l'occasion du centenaire de la naissance de Henri Bergson. *Bulletin de la Société française de Philosophie*, 54e année, janvier 1960, pp. 35-45.
Reprinted in *Signes*, "Bergson se faisant," pp. 229-241.
"Bergson in the Making," in *Signs*, pp. 182-191.
Another translation may be found in *The Bergsonian Heritage*, edited by Thomas Hanna. New York: Columbia University Press, 1962, pp. 133-149.

104   "La volonté dans la philosophie de Malebranche." [Séance du 19 décembre 1959] *Bulletin de la Société française de Philosophie*, 54e année, juillet-septembre 1960. [Intervention by Merleau-Ponty, pp. 133-134.]

105   "Préface" to *L'Oeuvre de Freud et son importance pour le monde moderne*, by Dr. A. Hesnard. Paris: Payot, 1960, pp. 5-10.
English trans. by Alden L. Fisher, "Phenomenology and Existentialism," pp. 81-87 in *The Essential Writings of Merleau-Ponty*.

106   "Entretien." *Les Ecrivains en personne*, par Madeleine Chapsal. Paris: Julliard, 1960, pp. 145-163.

107   "Husserl aux limites de la phénoménologie." (cours du lundi),

108   "Nature et Logos: le corps humain," (cours du jeudi). *Annuaire du Collège de France*, 60e année, 1960-61, pp. 169-173, 173-176.
Reprinted in *Résumés de cours*, pp. 159-170, 171-180.
"Husserl at the Limits of Phenomenology," and "Nature and Logos: the Human Body," in *Themes from the Collège de France*, pp. 113-123, 124-131.

109   *Signes*. Paris: Gallimard, 1960. 438 pp. Collection of the following articles with a Preface dated 'February and September 1960':

   Part I Introduction
   Part II
      1- Indirect Language and the Voices of Silence (Nos. 56 and 57)
      2- On the Phenomenology of Language (No. 54)
      3- The Philosopher and Sociology (No. 51)
      4- From Mauss to Claude Lévi-Strauss (No. 101)
      5- Everywhere and Nowhere (No. 86)
      6- The Philosopher and His Shadow (No. 100)
      7- Bergson in the Making (No. 103)
      8- Einstein and the Crisis of Reason (No. 77)
      9- Reading Montaigne (No. 31)
      10- A Note on Machiavelli (No. 42)
      11- Man and Adversity (No. 53)
   Part III
      1- Paranoid Politics (No. 39)
      2- Marxism and Superstition (No. 43)
      3- The U.S.S.R. and the Camps (No. 45)
      4- The Yalta Papers (No. 75)
      5- The Future of the Revolution (No. 80)
      6- On De-Stalinization (No. 89)
      7- On Eroticism (No. 63)
      8- On News Items (No. 67)
      9- On Claudel (No. 73)
      10- On Abstaining (No. 79)
      11- On Indo-China (No. 97)
      12- On Madagascar (Interview) (No. 96)
      13- On May 13, 1958 (No. 94)
      14- Tomorrow... (Interview) (No. 95)
   English trans. by Richard C. McCleary. *Signs*. Evanston, Illinois: Northwestern University Press, 1964.
   Spanish trans. by G. Martinez y G. Oliver. *Signos*. Barcelona: Seix Barral, 1964. (Biblioteca breve. Ciencias Humanas, 199).
   Italian trans. by A. Bonomi. *Segni*. Milano: Il Saggiatore, 1967.
   Portuguese trans. by F. Gil. *Sinais*. Lisboa: Minotauro, 1962.

110   "La philosophie et la politique sont solidaires." [interview with J.-P. Weber.] *Le Monde*, 31 décembre 1960.

1961

111   "L'oeil et l'esprit." [dated juillet-août 1960.] *Art de France*, no. 1, janvier 1961, pp. 187-208.
Reprinted in *Les Temps Modernes*, 17e année, 1961-62, no. 184-185, numéro spécial, octobre 1961, pp. 193-227.
In book form, *L'Oeil et l'esprit*. Paris: Gallimard 1964. 93 pp.
[The article as originally published and as reprinted in book form contains illustrations chosen by Merleau-Ponty.]
English trans. by Carleton Dallery in James M. Edie, ed., *The Primacy of Perception and Other Essays*, 1964, pp. 159-190. Also in Alden Fisher, *The Essential Writings of Merleau-Ponty*, pp. 252-286.
German trans. by H. W. Arnd. *Das Auge und der Geist. Philosophische Essays*. Hamburg: Rowohlt, 1967.
Italian trans. by G. Invitto. *L'occhio e lo spirito*. Lecce: Milella, 1971.
Portuguese trans. by G. Dantas Barreto. *O ôlho e o espirito*. Rio de Janeiro: Grifo ed. 1969.

112   "L'ontologie cartésienne et l'ontologie d'aujourd'hui: Philosophie et non-philosophie depuis Hegel [textes commentés]." *Annuaire du Collège de France*, p. 163. 61e année, 1961-62, p. 16. [Subjects treated in his last courses at the Collège de France.]

113   "Cinq notes sur Claude Simon." *Méditations, Revue des expressions contemporaines*, no. 4, 1961, pp. 5-10. [Contains: 1- "Vision, octobre 1960; 2- "Langage, Claude Simon, Butor," octobre 1960; 3- "Claude Simon et l'intégration 'verticale'," novembre 1960; 4- "Claude Simon," 19 décembre 1960; 5- "L'association comme initiation," mars 1961.]

1962

114   "La phénoménologie contre 'The Concept of Mind'." *La philosophie analytique*, Cahiers de Royaumont (Philosophie: IV). Paris: Editions de Minuit, 1962, pp. 65-84. Discussion, pp. 85-104. Merleau Ponty's intervention, pp. 93-96.

115 "Un inédit de Maurice Merleau-Ponty." *Revue de Métaphysique et de Morale*, 67e année, 1962, octobre 1962, no. 4, pp. 401-409. [Exposé pour sa candidature au Collège de France dating from 1952.] English trans. by Arleen B. Dallery, "An Unpublished Text by Maurice Merleau-Ponty: A Prospectus of his Work," pp. 3-11 in James E. Edie, ed., *The Primacy of Perception and Other Essays*, 1964. Also in Alden Fisher, *The Essential Writings of Merleau-Ponty* pp. 367-376. [A personal communication to Martial Gueroult written by Merleau-Ponty in 1952 at the time of his candidacy to the Collège de France, when Gueroult was putting together a report of his qualifications for presentation to the assembly of professors.] German trans. by A. Metraux, "Schrift für die Kandidatur am Collège de France," in *Vorlesungen I*. Berlin, New York: de Gruyter, 1973.

116 Colloque sur le mot structure, in *Sens et usages du terme structure dans les sciences humaines et sociales*. S-Graven-Hage: Mouton, 1962, pp. 153-155, 156-157.

117 Van Breda, H. L. "Maurice Merleau-Ponty et les Archives-Husserl à Louvain." *Revue de Métaphysique et de Morale*, 67e année, 1962, pp. 412, 413, 420, 421-422, 429-430. [Fragments of letters written by Merleau-Ponty to Van Breda.]

118 *Le Visible et l'invisible*, suivi de notes de travail. Texte établi par Claude Lefort, accompagné d'un avertissement et d'une postface. Paris: Gallimard, 1964. 362 pp.
English trans. by A. Lingus, *The Visible and the Invisible*. Evanston, Illinois: Northwestern University Press, 1968.
Spanish trans. by J. Escudé, *Lo Visible y lo invisible*. Barcelona: Seix Barral, 1970.
Italian trans. by A. Bonomi, *Lo Visibile e l'invisibile*. Milano: Bompiani, 1969.

119 *Maurice Merleau-Ponty à la Sorbonne*. Résumé de ses cours établi par des étudiants et approuvé par lui-même. *Bulletin de Psychologie*, Tome XVIII, novembre 1964, pp. 109-336. Contains:
1- "Méthode en psychologie de l'enfant," (1951-52), pp. 109-140;
2- "Les sciences de l'homme et la phénoménologie," (1950-52), pp. 141-170.
English trans., "Phenomenology and the sciences of man," in James M. Edie, ed., *The Primacy of Perception and Other Essays*, 1964.
German trans., A. Metraux, in *Vorlesungen, I*. Berlin, New York: de Gruyter, 1973.

3- "Structure et conflits de la conscience enfantine," (1949-1950), pp. 171-202.
4- "Psychosociologie de l'enfant," (1950-1951), pp. 203-225;
5- "La conscience et l'acquisition du langage," (1949-1950), pp. 226-259.
English trans. by Hugh J. Silverman, *Consciousness and the Acquisition of Language*. Evanston, Illinois: Northwestern University Press, 1973, 108 pp.
6- "Les relations avec autrui chez l'enfant," (1950-1951), pp. 205-336.
English trans., "The child's relations with Others," in James M. Edie, ed., *The Primacy of Perception and Other Essays*, 1964.

1965

120   "Husserl et la notion de nature." Notes prises au cours du 14 et 25 mars 1957, par Xavier Tilliette. *Revue de Métaphysique et de Morale*, 70e année, no. 3, 1965, pp. 259-269.

1966

121   "La philosophie de l'existence." [Lecture given in 1959 at the Maison canadienne de la cité universitaire de Paris.] *Dialogue*, vol. V, no. 3, 1966, pp. 307-322.

1967

122   "Pages d'Introduction à la *Prose du Monde*." [first pages of an incomplete manuscript and presented by Claude Lefort.] *Revue de Métaphysique et de Morale*, 72e année, no. 2, 1967, pp. 139-153.

123   "Commenté par Merleau-Ponty." [On Claude Simon.] *Le Monde [des Livres]*, no. 6932, 26 avril, 1967, p. 5.

1968

124   *Résumés de Cours*, Collège de France 1952-1960. Avertissement par Claude Lefort. Paris: Gallimard, 1968. 180pp.

English trans. by John O'Neill, *Themes from the Lectures at the Collège de France 1952-1960*. Evanston, Illinois: Northwestern University Press, 1970. 131p.
Spanish trans. by H. Acevedo, *Filosofia y lenguaje: resumenes de los cursos del Collège de France*. Buenos Aires: Proteo, 1969.
German trans. by A. Metraux, "Vorlesungszusammenfassungen: Collège de France 1952-1960," in *Vorlesungen I*. Berlin, New York: de Gruyter, 1973.

125   *L'union de l'âme et du corps chez Malebranche, Biran et Bergson*. Notes prises au cours de Maurice Merleau-Ponty à l'Ecole Normale Supérieure (1947-1948), recueillies et rédigées par Jean Deprun. Paris: Vrin, 1968. 118pp.

1969

126   *La Prose du monde*. Texte établi et présenté par Claude Lefort. Paris: Gallimard, 1969. 216pp.
English trans. by John O'Neill, *The Prose of the World*. Evanston, Illinois: Northwestern University Press, 1973. xlvi, 154 pp.
Spanish trans. by F. Gutíerez, *La Prosa del mundo*. Madrid: Taurus, 1971.

PART TWO

BIBLIOGRAPHY ON MERLEAU-PONTY

SECTION ONE: BOOKS (Including book reviews)

A) BOOKS IN ENGLISH

127   Bannan, John F. *The Philosophy of Merleau-Ponty*. New York: Harcourt, Brace and World, 1967.

   Book Review:

128   George J. Stack, *Modern Schoolman*, vol. XXXXVI, 1968-69, pp. 155-156.

129   André Devaux, *Revue Philosophique de Louvain*, février 1972, pp. 309-310.

130   Barral, Mary Rose. *Merleau-Ponty. The Role of the Body-Subject in Interpersonal Relations*. Pittsburgh: Duquesne University Press, 1965.

   Book Review:

131   James Collins, *Cross Currents*, XVI, 1966, p. 186.

132   K. T. Gallagher, *International Philosophical Quarterly*, VI, 1966, pp. 768-769.

133   Warren Gorman, *The Psychoanalytic Review*, LV, no. 1, Spring 1968, pp. 152-153.

134   John O'Neill, *Philosophy and Phenomenological Research*, XXVII, 1966-67, pp. 624-625.

135   Gillan, Garth, ed. *The Horizons of the Flesh: Critical Perspectives on the Thought of Merleau-Ponty*. Carbondale, Ill.: Southern Illinois University Press, 1973. [Contains essays by G. Gillan, "In the Folds of the Flesh: Philosophy and Language," pp. 1-60; D. Ihde, "Singing the world: Language and perception," pp. 61-77; A. Lingus, "Being in the interrogative mood," pp. 78-91; R. Herbenick, "Merleau-Ponty and the primacy of reflection," pp. 92-113; B. Flynn, "The question of ontology: Sartre and Merleau-Ponty," pp. 114-126; J. Bien, "Merleau-Ponty's conception of history," pp. 127-142; D. Howard, "Ambiguous radicalism: Merleau-Ponty's interrogation of political thought," pp. 143-159; R. Bruzina, "Merleau-Ponty and Husserl: the idea of science," pp. 160-174.

34   BOOKS

  Book Review:

136   Barry Cooper, *Canadian Journal of Political Science*, vol. VII, no. 4, 1974, pp. 725-726.

137   Duwayne Engelhardt, *Review of Metaphysics*, vol. XXVII, March 1974, pp. 610-611.

138   Kaelin, Eugene. *An Existentialist Aesthetics: The Theories of Sartre and Merleau-Ponty*. Madison, Wisconsin: The University of Wisconsin Press, 1962. 417p.

139   Kwant, Remy C. *The Phenomenological Philosophy of Merleau-Ponty*. Pittsburgh: Duquesne University Press, 1963. [Trans. from the Dutch by Henry Koren.]

  Book Review:

140   F. C. Copleston, *The Heytrop Journal*, vol. VI, 1965, pp. 72-74.

141   M. Vanhoutte, *Revue Philosophique de Louvain*, LXIV, 1966, pp. 322-325.

142   Kwant, Remy C. *From Phenomenology to Metaphysics. An Inquiry into the Last Period of Merleau-Ponty's Philosophical Life*. Pittsburgh: Duquesne University Press, 1966.

  Book Review:

143   T. W. Busch, *International Philosophical Quarterly*, vol. VII, no. 4, Dec. 1967, pp. 681-685.

144   André Devaux, *Revue Philosophique de Louvain*, February 1972, pp. 150-152.

145   Thomas Langan, *Philosophy and Phenomenological Research*, vol. XXVIII, 1968-69, pp. 606-607.

146   Langan, Thomas. *Merleau-Ponty's Critique of Reason*. New Haven: Yale University Press, 1966.

  Book Review:

147   T. W. Busch, *New Scholasticism*, vol. XXXXIII, 1969, pp. 324-327.

148   A. Medina, *Man and World*, vol. I, 1968, pp. 303-309.

149   A. Paskow, *Review of Metaphysics*, vol. XXI, 1967-68, pp. 554-555.

150   Mary Warnock, *New Society*, vol. IX, no. 228, Feb. 9, 1967, p. 212.

151   Lanigan, Richard L. *Speaking and Semiology: Maurice Merleau-Ponty's Phenomenological Theory of Existential Communication*. The Hague: Mouton, 1972. 257 p. (bib. p. [210]-243). Approaches to semiotics, 22.

Book Review:

152   Gerald J. Carruba, *Kinesis*, vol. VI, no. 1, Fall 1973, pp. 56-61.

153   O'Neill, John. *Perception, Expression and History: The Social Phenomenology of M. Merleau-Ponty*. Evanston, Ill.: Northwestern University Press, 1970.

Book Review:

154   Joseph Bien, *Dialogue*, vol. XI, March 1972, pp. 162-164.

155   Stephan T. Mayo, *International Philosophical Quarterly*, vol. XIII, March 1973, pp. 154-155.

156   Rabil, Albert. *Merleau-Ponty: Existentialist of the Social World*. New York: Columbia University Press, 1967.

Book Review:

157   R. Maloney, *The Heytrop Journal*, Vol. X, 1969, pp. 84-86.

158   Pierre Dubois, *Revue Philosophique de la France et de l'Etranger*, CLXI, no. 4, 1971, pp. 504-507.

159   James M. Edie, *Journal of Value Inquiry*, vol. II, 1968, pp. 216-225.

160   Colin Smith, *Philosophical Quarterly*, vol. XIX, 1969, pp. 362-363.

161   Sallis, John. *Phenomenology and the Return to Beginnings*. (Philosophical Series, no. 32). Pittsburgh: Duquesne University Press, distributed by Humanities Press, New York, 1973.

Book Review:

162   R. R. E. *Review of Metaphysics*, vol. XXVII, 1973-1974.

36   BOOKS

163   James E. Hansen, *Philosophy and Phenomenological Research*, vol. XXXV, no. 3, March 1975, pp. 432-433.

164   Michael E. Zimmermann, *International Philosophical Quarterly*, vol. XV, no. 2, June 1975, pp. 241-244.

165   Zaner, Richard M. *The Problem of Embodiment. Some Contributions to a Phenomenology of the Body*. The Hague: Martinus Nijhoff, 1964, pp. 127-238.

            Book Review:

166   A. Deregibus, *Giornale di Metafisica*, XXI, 1966, pp. 442-446.

167   E.A.R. *Review of Metaphysics*, XIX, 1965-1966, pp. 604-605.

            B) <u>BOOKS IN FRENCH</u>

168   Charron, Ghyslain. *Du Langage. A. Martinet et M. Merleau-Ponty*. Ottawa: Editions de l'Université d'Ottawa, 1972. 187p. (bib. p. 175-184). Coll. Philsoophica, no. 1.

            Book Review:

169   James M. Edie, *The Thomist*, vol. XXXVII, Oct. 1973, pp. 807-811.

170   Gilles Lane, *Dialogue*, vol. XII, no. 2, June 1973, pp. 390-392.

171   Jean Theau, *Revue de l'Université d'Ottawa*, vol. XLIII, 1973, pp. 627-628.

171a   Fontaine de Visscher, Luce. *Phénomène ou structure? Essai sur le langage chez Merleau-Ponty*. Bruxelles: Publications Universitaires Saint-Louis, 1974.

            Book Review:

171b   J.-P. Cotten, *Revue de Métaphysique et de Morale*, tome LXXX, janvier-mars, 1975, pp. 127-130.

172   Fressin, Augustin. *La Perception chez Bergson et Merleau-Ponty*. Paris: S.E.D.E.S., 1967, 344p.

Book Review:

173 Antoon Burgers, *Tijdschrift voor Filosofie*, vol. XXX, 1968, pp. 416-418.

174 Th. Quonian, *Les Etudes Philosophiques*, 1968, pp. 68-69.

175 Garaudy, R. et al. *Mésaventures de l'antimarxisme. Les malheurs de M. Merleau-Ponty.* Receuil de textes, accompagné d'une lettre de Georg Lukács. Paris: Editions Sociales, 1956. 160p. [On *Les Aventures de la dialectique* (1955). Contains: R. Garaudy, "Aventures de la dialectique ou dialectique d'une aventure?", pp. 7-98; H. Lefebvre, "Une philosophie de l'ambigüité," pp. 99-106; J. T. Desanti, "Retour à Berkeley," pp. 107-124; M. Caveing, "Pragmatisme et pratique," pp. 125-132; V. Leduc, "Il n'y a pas de 'gauche' anticommuniste," pp. 133-141; J. Kanapa, "Avec qui êtes-vous, maîtres de la culture?", pp. 142-148; G. Cogniot, "Conclusions," pp. 149-157; G. Lukács, "Lettre de G. Lukács à la rédaction des *Cahiers du Communisme*," pp. 158-160.]

176 Geraets, Théodore F. *Vers une nouvelle philosophie transcendantale. La genèse de la philosophie de Maurice Merleau-Ponty jusqu'à la 'Phénoménologie de la perception'.* Préface par Emmanuel Lévinas. (Phaenomenologica, 39). The Hague: Martinus Wijhoff, 1971, xv-212p.

Book Review:

177 Garth Gillan, *Philosophy and Phenomenological Research*, vol. XXXV, no. 1, Sept. 1974, pp. 135-137.

178 Alexandre Métraux, *Archives de Philosophie*, tome XXXVIII, cahier 1, janvier-mars 1975, pp. 161-164.

179 Claude Panaccio, *Dialogue*, vol. XI, Dec. 1972, pp. 615-619.

179a Gary B. Madison, *Philosophiques*, vol. II, avril 1975, pp. 103-112.

179b Théodore F. Geraets, *Philosophiques*, vol. II, avril 1975, pp. 128-130.

180 Halda, Bernard. *Merleau-Ponty ou la philosophie de l'ambigüité.* (Archives des lettres modernes, 72). Paris: Les Lettres Modernes, 1966. 64p. Paris: Minard, 1967.

38   BOOKS

181   Heldsieck, François. *L'Ontologie de Merleau-Ponty.*
      Paris: Presses Universitaires de France, 1971.
      143p. (Bibliothèque de philosophie contempo-
      raine).

      Book Review:

182   Dominique Rey, *Revue de Théologie et de Philo-
      sophie*, no. 4, 1972, pp. 255-264.

183   Xavier Tilliette, *Etudes*, tome 336, janvier-juin
      1972, p. 160.

184   Hyppolite, Jean. *Sens et existence dans la philo-
      sophie de Maurice Merleau-Ponty.* Oxford at the
      Clarendon Press, 1963. [Zaharoff Lecture for 1963]
      Reprinted in vol. 2, pp. 731-758, in *Figures de la
      pensée philosophique. Ecrits (1931-1968).* Paris:
      Presses Universitaires de France, 1971.

      Book Review:

185   Remo Tapalla, *Rivista Filosofica Neo-Scolastica*,
      vol. LXV, July-sept. 1973, pp. 617-619.

186   Madison, Gary Brent. *La Phénoménologie de Merleau-
      Ponty. Une recherche des limites de la conscience.*
      Préface de Paul Ricoeur (Publications de l'Uni-
      versité de Paris X Nanterre. Lettres et Sciences
      Humaines, série A: Thèses et Travaux, 20). Paris:
      Klincksieck, 1973, 284p.

      Book Review:

186a Theodore F. Geraets, *Philosophiques*, vol. II,
      avril 1975, pp. 113-123.

186b Gary B. Madison, *Philosophiques*, vol. II, avril
      1972, pp. 123-128.

187   Meddens, Hans. *Une Phénoménologie du corps. La
      notion du corps trouvée par la phénoménologie de
      Merleau-Ponty enrichissant l'intelligence de la
      notion classique d'habitus.* Rome: Pontificia
      Universita Gregoriana, 1965. Bruxelles: Ed.
      Meddens, 1966.

188   Moreau, Joseph. *L'Horizon des esprits. Essai cri-
      tique sur 'La Phénoménologie de la perception'.*
      Paris: Presses Universitaires de France, 1960.

      Book Review:

189   A. Deregibus, *Giornale di Metafisica*, no. 5, 1961,
      pp. 678-682.

190 Robinet, André. *Merleau-Ponty, sa vie, son oeuvre, avec un exposé de sa philosophie.* (Collection "Philosophes"). Paris: Presses Universitaires de France, 1963. 124p. 2nd. ed. revised and updated, 1970.

Book Review:

191 Enrico Sturani, *Rivista di Filosofia*, vol. LV, no. 3, 1964, pp. 350-352.

192 Szaszkiewicz, Jerzy (Georgius). *Relation entre le comportement et la connaissance selon Merleau-Ponty: Intelligence, liberté et réflexion.* Roma: Tipografia Pontificiae Universitatis Gregorianae, 1962. 103p.

193 Tilliette, Xavier. *Philosophes contemporains: G. Marcel, M. Merleau-Ponty, K. Jaspers.* Paris: Desclée de Brouwer, 1962. [Merleau-Ponty, pp. 49-86.]

194 Tilliette, Xavier. *Le Corps et le temps dans la 'Phénoménologie de la perception'.* Bale: Verlag für Recht und Gesellschaft, 1964. 16p.

195 Tilliette, Xavier. *Existence et littérature.* Paris: Desclée de Brouwer, 1962, 205p.

196 Tiliette, Xavier. *Maurice Merleau-Ponty ou la mesure de l'homme.* Paris: Seghers, 1970. 188p. Coll. "Philosophes de tous les temps," no. 64.

Book Review:

197 Michel Sales, *Archives de Philosophie*, tome 34, janvier-mars 1971, pp. 167-168.

198 Michel Sales, *Etudes*, octobre 1970, pp. 443-445.

199 Waelhens, Alphonse de. *Une Philosophie de l'ambiguïté. L'existentialisme de Maurice Merleau-Ponty.* Louvain: Publications Universitaires de Louvain, 1st ed. 1951; 3rd rev. ed., 1968; 4th ed. 1971.

Book Review:

200 Roland Caillois, *Critique*, vol. VIII, no. 58, mars 1952, pp. 284-286.

201 James Collins, *The Modern Schoolman*, vol. XXIX, 1951-52, pp. 52-55.

BOOKS

202   Albert Dondeyne, *Tijdschrift voor Filosofie*, vol. XIV, 1952, pp. 744-747.

203   B. R. *Rivista Internazionale di Filosofia del Diritto*, vol. XXXXV, 1968, pp. 169-170. [Review of 3rd ed.]

C) BOOKS IN GERMAN

204   Brand, G. *Die Lebenswelt. Eine Philosophie des konkretes Apriori.* Berlin: Walter de Gruyter, 1970. [Chapter 5: Merleau-Ponty, pp. 164-201.]

205   Juritsch, Martin. *Sinn und Geist. Ein Beitrag zur Deutung der Sinne in der Einheit des Menschen.* Fribourg, Switzerland: Universitätsverlag, 1961. [Merleau-Ponty, pp. 77-162.]

206   Maier, Willi. *Das Problem der Leiblickheit bei Jean-Paul Sartre und Maurice Merleau-Ponty.* (Forschungen zur Paedagogik und Anthropologie, 7). Tübingen: Niemeyer Verlag, 1964. xiii-104p.

207   Pilz, Georg M. *Maurice Merleau-Ponty. Ontologie und Wissenschaftskritik* (Abhandlungen zur Philosophie, Psychologie und Pädagogik, 83). Bonn: Bouvier, 1973, 142p.

208   Plügge, Hans. *Das Mensch und sein Leib.* Tübingen: Niemeyer Verlag, 1967.

209   Podlech, Adalbert. *Der Leib als Weise des in-der-Welt-Seins: Eine Systematische Arbeit innerhalb der phänomenologischen Existenz-Philosophie.* Bonn: Bouvier, 1956. 250p.

D) BOOKS IN ITALIAN

210   Bonomi, Andrea. *Esistenza e strutturà. Saggio su Merleau-Ponty.* (La Cultura, Biblioteca di Filosofia, Psicologia e Scienze Umane). Milano: Il Saggiatore, 1967. 253p.

Book Review:

211   P. Cardoletti, *La Scuola Cattolica*, tome LXXXVII, 1969, supp. bib. pp. 142-144.

212 A. Dentoni, *Giornale di Metafisica*, vol. XXVI, 1971, pp. 112-114.

213 Giorgio Derossi, *Filosofia*, vol. XIX, 1968, pp. 448-451.

214 Alessandra Greppi, *Humanitas*, vol. XXIII, 1968, pp. 802-803.

215 Giuseppe Patella, *Giornale Critico della Filosofia Italiana*, vol. XXIII, july-sept. 1969, pp. 469-475.

216 S. Pucella, *Dialogue*, vol. VII, 1968-69, pp. 511-513.

217 Brena, Gian Luigi. *La struttura della percezioni. Studio su Merleau-Ponty.* (Pubblicazioni dell'Università Cattolica dell'Sacro Cuore, Saggi e ricerche. Series 3. Scienze filosofische, 5). Milano: Vita e Pensiero, 1969. xi-201p.

Book Review:

218 G. Avesani, *Gregoriamum*, vol. LI, 1970, pp. 575-576.

219 M. Lencci, *Rivista Filosofia Neo-Scolastica*, vol. LXIII, Jan.-April 1971, pp. 220-221.

220 Giuseppe Nicoloci, *Giornale di Metafisica*, vol. XXVII, March-June 1972, pp. 277-279.

221 Giuseppe Patella, *Filosofia*, vol. XXI, Jan. 1970, pp. 101-104.

222 Centineo, Ettore. *Una fenomenologia della storia. L'esistenzialismo di Maurice Merleau-Ponty.* Palermo: Palumbe ed. Capucci e Figli, 1959. 158p.

Book Review:

223 G. Masi, *Giornale di Metafisica*, no. 5, 1960, pp. 655-659.

224 Derossi, Giorgio. *Maurice Merleau-Ponty* (Filosofi d'oggi). Torino: Edizioni di 'Filosofia', 1965. 130p.

Book Review:

225 M. A. Raschini, *Giornale di Metafisica*, XXI, 1966, pp. 744-746.

42   BOOKS

226   Invitto, Giovanni. *Merleau-Ponty politico: l'eresia programmatica* (Biblioteca di ricerca politica, 1). Manduria: Lacaita, 1971, 127p.

Book Review:

227   L. Bírtolo, *Filosofia*, vol. XXIV, 1973, pp. 238-240.

228   L. Bírtolo, *Ethica*, vol. XII, 1973, pp. 76-78.

229   Penati, Giancarlo. *Ontologia e critica del concreto. Lavelle e Merleau-Ponty*. Milano: Marzorati, 1970. 218p.

230   Semerari, Giuseppe. *Da Schelling a Merleau-Ponty: studi sulla filosofia contemporanea*. Bologna: Cappelli, 1962. 422 p. [Merleau-Ponty, pp. 245-382.]

231   Senofonte, Ciro. *Sartre e Merleau-Ponty* (Università degli studi di Salerno. Collana di studi e testi, 9). Napoli: Libreria Scientifica Editrice, 1972. 290p.

232   Toscono, Giuseppe. *Percezione, linguaggio, comunicazione. Saggio su Merleau-Ponty* (Cultura e tempo, 2). Catania: N. Giannotta, 1972. 237p.

Book Review:

233   Rosario V. Cristaldi, *Rivista di Studi Crociani*, vol. X, Jan.-March 1973, pp. 112-113.

E)   BOOKS IN SPANISH

234   Delfino, R. *Cuerpo y alma en Merleau-Ponty*. Buenos Aires: Pellegrini, 1964.

Book Review:

235   T. Alesanco, *Crisis*, XII, 1965, pp. 410-411.

236   S. Contu, *Rivista Rosminiani di Filosofia e di Cultura*, LX' 1966, pp. 302-303.

237   A. Guy, *Etudes Philosophiques*, XXI, 1966, pp. 84-85.

238   X. Tilliette, *Archives de Philosophie*, XXIX, 1966, p. 157.

BOOKS   43

239   Ibañez Martín Mellado, José Antonio. *El compromiso humano en la historia en filosofía de M. Merleau-Ponty*. Madrid: Facultad de Filosofía y Letras, 1973, 36p.

240   Masotta, O. *Conciencia y estructura*. Buenos Aires: J. Alvarez, 1968.

241   Ollero Tassara, Andrés. *Dialéctica y praxis en Merleau-Ponty*. Granada: Universidad de Granada, Faculdad de Derecho, 1971. 164p.

Book Review:

242   Anonymous. *Anales Catedra Suarez*, vol. XI, 1971, pp. 165-166.

243   D. Pecilli, *Rivista Internazionale di Filosofia del Diritto*, vol. L, 1973, pp. 355-356.

244   Ravagnan, Luis Maria. *Merleau-Ponty*. (Col. Enciclopedia del pensamiento esencial). Buenos Aires: Centro Editor de America Latina, 1967. 116p.

245   Touron del Pie, Eliseo. *El hombre, el mundo y Dios en la fenomenología de Merleau-Ponty*. Madrid: Revista Estudio. Dist. difusora del Libro, 1961, 99p. Publ. del Monasterio de Poyo.

Book Review:

246   V. Capanaga, *Augustinus*, VII, 1962, pp. 481-482.

247   Yagüe, Joaquín. *M. Merleau-Ponty y la fenomenología*. Madrid: Libreria Editorial Augustinus, 1971. 155p. (bib. p. [137]-155).

Book Review:

248   Emiliano Aguado, *Estafeta Literaria*, num. 477, Oct. 1, 1971, p. 718.

F)   BOOKS IN DUTCH

249   Bakker, Reinout. *Merleau-Ponty* (Wijsgerige monografieen). Onder red. van B. Delfgaauw, G. R. Nuchelmans en J. Sperna Weiland. Baarn: Het Wereldvenster, 1965. 128p.

BOOKS

250 Bakker, Reinout. *Noodzakelijke samenwerking. Merleau-Pontys bijdrage tot het gesprek tussen filosofie en wetenschapp.* Groningen: Wolters; Antwerpen: Noord-Nederlands Boekbedrijk, 1965. 26p.

251 Bakker, Reinout. *Merleau-Ponty* [en zijn betekenis voor onze tijd]. Herdruck. Baarn: Het Werensvenster, 1970.

252 Kwant, Remy C. *De fenomenologie van Merleau-Ponty.* Utrecht: Het Spectrum, 1962. [English trans. by Henry Koren, *The Phenomenological Philosophy of Merleau-Ponty.* Pittsburgh: Duquesne University Press, 1963.]

253 Kwant, Remy C. *De stemmen der stilte. Merleau-Ponty's analyse van de schilderkunst.* Hilversum Antwerpen: Paul Brand, 1966. 146p.

254 Kwant, Remy C. *Mens en expressie in het licht van de wijsbegeerte van Merleau-Ponty.* Antwerp-Utrecht: Aula-Boeken Uitgeverij "Het Spectrum", 1968. 185p.

255 Kwant, Remy C. *De wijsbegeerte van Merleau-Ponty.* Antwerpen-Utrecht: Aula-Boeken Uitgeverij "Het Spectrum", 1968. 360p. [An enlarged edition of previous reference.]

256 Struyker Boudier, C. E. M. *Fenomenologie en psychoanalyse: de problematiek van het bewustzijn en de psychoanalyse bij Maurice Merleau-Ponty.* Tilburg: Gianotten, 1970.

G) BOOK IN NORWEGIAN

257 Stubberud, Tore. *Det litteraere uttrykk: En studie i Merleau-Pontys fenomenologi.* Oslo: Tanum, 1972. 242p.

SECTION TWO: DOCTORAL DISSERTATIONS

258 Albert, Hughes. "Histoire et historicité chez Maurice Merleau-Ponty." Thèse Université de Strasbourg. Lettres. 1968. (Dactylographie. 334p.)

259 Arras, John Dyer. "A criticism of existentialist ethics." Northwestern University. *Dissertation Abstracts*, vol. 33, no. 10, April 1973, pp. 5771-5772-A.

260 Barral, Mary Rose. "Merleau-Ponty: The role of the body in interpersonal relations." Fordham University, 1963. *Dissertation Abstracts*, vol. 24, no. 3, April 1963, p. 1200-A.

261 Berger, Carol Altekruse. "Merleau-Ponty on the relations of body and soul." Saint Louis University, 1973. *Dissertation Abstracts*, vol. 34, 1973-74, p. 5239-A.

262 Besson, Françoise Gisèle. "La doctrine cartésienne des relations de l'âme et du corps à la lumière de la lecture qu'en donne Maurice Merleau-Ponty." Thèse de doctorat, 1971-72, Université Catholique de Louvain.

263 Bertoldi, Eugene. "Merleau-Ponty and the phenomenology of phenomenology." University of Waterloo (Canada), 1973. *Dissertation Abstracts*, vol. 34, April 1974, pp. 6695-A.

264 Bertram, Maryane J. "Subjectivity in the monism of Merleau-Ponty." Marquette University, 1971. *Dissertation Abstracts*, vol. 32, no. 8, Feb. 1972, p. 4655-A.

265 Bettler, Alan Raymond. "A chronicle of the beginnings of French existentialism." *Dissertation Abstracts*, vol. 31, no. 5, Nov. 1970, p. 2432-A.

266 Bien, Joseph. "Le marxisme et la question de la terreur chez Merleau-Ponty." Thèse 3e cycle. Nanterre. Lettres. 1968. (Dactylographié. 225p.)

DISSERTATIONS

267   Bruzina, Ronald C. "Logos and Eidos: A Study in the phenomenological meaning of 'concept' according to Husserl and Merleau-Ponty." University of Notre Dame, 1966. 256p. *Dissertation Abstracts*, vol. 27, 1966, p. 1862-A.

268   Burgers, Antoon. "De perceptie bij Bergson en Merleau-Ponty." Louvain, 1964, vii-303p. (Katholieke Universiteit te Leuven. Hoger Instituut voor Wijsbegeerte: Thesis voor het Doctoraat in de Wijsbegeerte).

269   Busch, T. W. "The role of the cogito in the philosophy of Maurice Merleau-Ponty." Marquette University, 1967. 178p. *Dissertation Abstracts*, vol. 28, no. 11, 1968, p. 4661-A.

270   Cantwell, O. F. "Merleau-Ponty. Toward a phenomenological psychology of real knowledge." Catholic University of America, 1966. 233p. *Dissertation Abstracts*, vol. 27, 1967, p. 3076-A.

271   Carruba, Gerald J. "Merleau-Ponty and Volosinov: A phenomenological prolegomenon to a Marxist semiotic." Southern Illinois University, 1975.

272   Cobb, R. Ellen. "The Cartesian principle of self-evidence and Merleau-Ponty's thesis that 'I am my body'." University of Toronto, 1974.

273   Cooper, Fraser B. "Existential phenomenology and Marxism: The politics of Maurice Merleau-Ponty." Duke University, 1969. *Dissertation Abstracts*, vol. 31, no. 5, 1970, p. 2452-A.

274   Cunningham, Suzanne M. "Language and intersubjectivity in the phenomenology of Edmund Husserl." Florida State University. *Dissertation Abstracts*, vol. 33, no. 5, Nov. 1972, p. 2423-A.

275   Dallery, Robert Carleton. "Philosophy as integrative speech. Studies in Plato and Merleau-Ponty, with an Appendix: A translation of Merleau-Ponty's *L'Oeil et l'esprit*." Yale University, 1968. 328p. *Dissertation Abstracts*, vol. 30, Sept.-Oct. 1969, p. 1956-A.

276   Delfino, R. "Cuerpo y alma en Merleau-Ponty." Dissertatione ad lauream in Facultate Philosophica Sancti Michaelis. San Miguel, Argentina, 1964.

277   Dillon, Martin C. "Merleau-Ponty's ontology." Yale University, 1970. *Dissertation Abstracts*, vol. 31, no. 6, Dec. 1970, p. 2968-A.

278   Dreyfus, Hubert L. "Husserl's phenomenology of perception." Harvard University, 1964.

279   Dunne, R. "The validity of Merleau-Ponty's criticism of Sartre's Marxism." University of Ottawa, 1973.

280   Eisenberg, Allan Mark. "The function of the intentional body in Merleau-Ponty's *Phenomenology of perception*'." Columbia University, 1974. *Dissertation Abstracts*, vol. 35, no. 10, April 1975, p. 6759-A.

281   Fabian, Rainer. "Kontingenz und Sinngenesis. Zum Problem der Entfremdung und Geschichte bei Merleau-Ponty." University of Münster, 1973. 204p.

282   Fairchild, David Lawrence. "Merleau-Ponty and Austin: a study in philosophical method." Northwestern University, 1972. *Dissertation Abstracts*, vol. 33, no. 6, Dec. 1972, p. 2976-A.

283   Fressin, Augustin. "La perception chez Bergson et Merleau-Ponty. Thèse, 3e cycle. Lettres. Paris. 1966.

284   Friedman, Robert Malcolm. "The ontology of Maurice Merleau-Ponty." Columbia University, 1972. *Dissertation Abstracts*, vol. 35, no. 12, June 1975, p. 7957-A.

285   Froman, Wayne Jeffrey. "Merleau-Ponty: Language and the art of speech." Fordham University, 1975.

286   Gahamanyi, Célestin. "La conception de la liberté chez Jean-Paul Sartre et Maurice Merleau-Ponty." University of Fribourg, Switzerland, 1967. 223p.

287   Gallagher, Donald K. "Ontology and eidos: A critical study of Sartre and Merleau-Ponty." M. A. Thesis, University of Toledo, 1972.

288   Geraets, Theodore F. "La genèse de la philosophie de Merleau-Ponty jusqu'à la *Phénoménologie de la perception*'." Thèse. 3e cycle. Lettres. Paris. Nanterre, 1969.

289   Gillespie, M. L. "The problematic of Merleau-Ponty's *The Visible and the invisible*. Historical ontology." Southern Illinois University, Carbondale, 1974.

290   Good, Paul. "Du corps à la chair. Merleau-Ponty's Weg von der Phänomenologie zur 'Metaphysik'." University of Munchen, 1970. 258+XXIIIp.

DISSERTATIONS

291   Hamrick, William S. "Body, space, and time in the philosophies of Whitehead and Merleau-Ponty." Vanderbild University, 1971. *Dissertation Abstracts*, vol. 32, no. 5, Nov. 1971, p. 2742-A.

292   Hartley, John J. "The philosophy of Maurice Merleau-Ponty: A philosophy of form." University of Toronto, 1970. *Dissertation Abstracts*, vol. 32, no. 9, March 1972, p. 5285-A.

292a   Hogemann, Friedrick. "Das Problem der 'perception' in der phänomenologie de Merleau-Pontys." Univ. Köln, 1973. 300p.

293   Houghton, Giles K. "Merleau-Ponty: The genesis of objectivity in natural perception." The Catholic University of America, 1970. *Dissertation Abstracts*, vol. 31, no. 5, Nov. 1970, p. 2439-A.

294   Hunt, Sister Mary Michael. "Time in the philosophy of Merleau-Ponty." The Catholic University of Amrica, 1969. 292p. *Dissertation Abstracts*, vol. 30, no. 4, Oct. 1969, p. 1600-A.

295   Hurst, William J. "The self in the philosophy of Merleau-Ponty." Fordham University, 1974. *Dissertation Abstracts*, vol. 35, no. 5, Nov. 1974, p. 3057-A.

296   Ibañez Martín Mellado, José Antonio. "El compromiso humano con la historia en la filosofía de M. Merleaù-Ponty." Tesis doctoral, Madrid University, Facultad de Filosofía y Letras, 1973.

297   Jabbour, Victorine. "Descartes dans la philosophie de Merleau-Ponty, le 'cogito' et son interprétation phénoménologique." Thèse 3e cycle, Paris I, 1971. 245ff dactylographié.

298   Johanning, J. C. "The perception of persons: A comparison of recent approaches to the problem of other minds." Yale University, 1966. 220. *Dissertation Abstracts*, vol. 27, 1967, p. 3488-A.

299   Joseph, Audrey Benderman. "Artistic vision and the metaphysical imagination: Toward a phenomenology of aesthetic consciousness." University of New Mexico, 1974. *Dissertation Abstracts*, vol. 36, no. 3, Sept. 1975, p. 1580-A.

300   Kestenbaum, Victor. "An interpretation of Dewey's notion of habit from the perspective of Merleau-Ponty's phenomenology of the habitual body." Ed.D. diss., Rutgers University, 1972. *Dissertation Abstracts*, vol. 33, no. 4, Oct. 1972, p. 1782-A.

DISSERTATIONS

301   King, Thomas W. "Thinking, freedom, and intersubjectivity in the philosophy of Merleau-Ponty." The University of New Mexico, 1971. *Dissertation Abstracts*, vol. 32, no. 9, March 1972, p. 5287-A.

302   Langer, Monika Mechthilde. "Violence in the philosophy of Merleau-Ponty." University of Toronto, 1973. *Dissertation Abstracts*, vol. 35, no. 12, June 1975, p. 7961-A.

303   Lanigan, Richard L. "Speaking and semiology: Maurice Merleau-Ponty's phenomenological theory of existential communication." Southern Illinois University, 1969.

304   Lorenz, Hélène S. "Hierarchic man: Philosophy and the individual in the work of Maurice Merleau-Ponty." Tulane University, 1971. *Dissertation Abstracts*, vol. 32, no. 5, Nov. 1971, p. 2746-A.

305   Lowry, Atherton Clark. "The world of Merleau-Ponty." Fordham University, 1972. *Dissertation Abstracts*, vol. 34, no. 1, July 1973, p. 362-A.

306   MacGuigan, M. "The foundations of sexuality: Merleau-Ponty's conception of sexuality and its place in his philosophy." University of Ottawa, 1975.

307   Madison, Gary Brent. "La phénoménologie de Merleau-Ponty. Une recherche des limites de la conscience." Thèse, 3e cycle. Paris, Nanterre, 1972.

308   Mallin, Samuel B. "Merleau-Ponty's metaphysical epistemology." University of Toronto, 1974.

309   Manniello, Andrew. "The ontological status of intentionality in the philosophy of Maurice Merleau-Ponty." Fordham University, 1973. *Dissertation Abstracts*, vol. 35, no. 3, Sept. 1974, p. 1703-A.

310   Matukanga, Boniface. "Maurice Merleau-Ponty et l'histoire de son temps." Thèse 3e cycle. Nanterre. Lettres. 1968. (dactylographié).

311   Mayo, Stephan T. "Aftermath of the absolute. A study of contingency in the phenomenology of Merleau-Ponty." Fordham University, 1973. *Dissertation Abstracts*, vol. 35, no. 3, Sept. 1974, p. 1704-A.

312   McCleary, Richard Calverton. "Ambiguity and freedom in the philosophy of Merleau-Ponty." Film reproduction (M.A. Thesis). Chicago: University of Chicago Press, 1954.

DISSERTATIONS

313   Meddens, Hans. "Une phénoménologie du corps. La notion du corps trouvée par la phénoménologie de Merleau-Ponty enrichissant l'intelligence de la notion classique d'habitus." Pontificia Universita Gregoriana, Rome, 1965.

314   Minhinnick, J. "Merleau-Ponty's anti-Cartesianism, a type of moderate realism?" University of Ottawa, 1974.

315   Morriston, Charles Wesley. "Phenomenology and the problem of the external world." Northwestern University. *Dissertation Abstracts*, vol. 33, no. 10, April 1973, pp. 5779-5780-A.

316   Morgan, Kathryn Pauly. "Merleau-Ponty's critique of Descartes. An evaluation." The Johns Hopkins University, 1973, 509p. *Dissertation Abstracts*, vol. 34, 1973-74, pp. 7281-7282-A.

317   Murphy, Richard T. "Phenomenology and the dialectic: A study of prefeflexive consciousness in the phenomenological theories of Husserl, Sartre and Merleau-Ponty." Fordham University. *Dissertation Abstracts*, vol. 24, no. 2, Aug. 1963, pp. 779-780.

318   Park, Ynhui. "An ontological interpretation of the concept of expression in the philosophy of Merleau-Ponty." University of Southern California, 1970. *Dissertation Abstracts*, vol. 31, no. 12, 1971, p. 6663-A.

319   Pauls, Arleen Laura. "Existential political theory." University of Pittsburgh. *Dissertation Abstracts*, vol. 34, no. 5, Nov. 1973, p. 2725-A.

320   Pilz, Georg. "Maurice Merleau-Ponty. Ontologie und Wissenschaftskritik." Thesis, University Bonn, 1972.

321   Place, James Gordon. "Merleau-Ponty's philosophy of painting: A metaphysics of painting." Southern Illinois University, 1971. *Dissertation Abstracts*, vol. 32, no. 9, March 1972, p. 5296-A.

322   Purdy, Michael W. "Communication and institution in the phenomenology of Merleau-Ponty." Ohio University, 1973, 185p. *Dissertation Abstracts*, vol. 34, 1973-74, p. 2801-A.

323   Rabil, Albert. "Maurice Merleau-Ponty: The social philosophy of an existentialist humanist." Columbia University, 1964.

DISSERTATIONS 51

324 Rada Donath, Alejandro. "Fenomenologia y ontologia en Maurice Merleau-Ponty." Pontificio Ateneo Salesiano. Facolta di Filosofia, Roma, 1963. xxii-512p.

325 Rauch, Leo. "Intentionality and its development in the phenomenological psychology of Edmund Husserl." New York University, 1968, 241p. *Dissertation Abstracts*, vol. 29, 1968, pp. 937-938.

326 Robbins, Jack A. "Merleau-Ponty on Marxism 1945-1955: A dialectic of politics and philosophy." Fordham University, 1972. *Dissertation Abstracts*, vol. 33, no. 1, July 1972, p. 374-A.

327 Sandrini, F. "La fenomenologia di Merleau-Ponty e il rapporto dialettico." Université Catholique de Louvain, Institut Supérieur de Philosophie, 1957.

328 Sapontzis, Steve F. "Merleau-Ponty and philosophical methodology." Yale University, 1971. *Dissertation Abstracts*, vol. 32, no. 6, Dec. 1971, p. 3374-A.

329 Schouwers, Pierre E. "Conscience libre et morale selon Maurice Merleau-Ponty." St. Louis University, 1971. *Dissertation Abstracts*, vol. 32, no. 8, Feb. 1972, p. 4664-A.

330 Silverman, Hugh Jerald. "Existential ambiguity: A phenomenology of human nature." Stanford University. *Dissertation Abstracts*, vol. 34, no. 6, Dec. 1973, pp. 3472-3474-A.

331 Springer, W. C. "The world and the word in Merleau-Ponty. Toward an existential epistemology and an ontology of the human body." Rice University, 1967. 194p. *Dissertation Abstracts*, vol. 28, 1967-68, p. 1857-A.

332 Surkim, Marvin L. "Merleau-Ponty and the phenomenological critique of political science." New York University. *Dissertation Abstracts*, vol. 33, no. 11, May 1973, p. 6423-A.

333 Szaszkiewicz, Jerzy (Georgius). "Relation entre le comportement et la connaissance selon Merleau-Ponty: intelligence, liberté et réflexion." Facultate Philosophica Pontificiae Universitatis Gregorianae, Roma, 1962.

334 Taylor, Darrell. "Husserl and Merleau-Ponty on the problem of the cultural studies." University of Southern California, 1966. 424 p. *Dissertation Abstracts*, vol. 27, no. 2, Aug. 1966, p. 508-A.

DISSERTATIONS

335 Traub, Essen O. "The socio-political dimension of Merleau-Ponty's phenomenology." Bryn Mawr College. *Dissertation Abstracts*, vol. 34, April 1974, p. 6706-A.

336 Turner, Ingrid Jacqueline. "Maurice Merleau-Ponty: The philosophy of language." Columbia University, 1974. *Dissertation Abstracts*, vol. 35, no. 10, April 1975, p. 6765-A.

337 Walsh, Margaret Ann. "foundational sexuality: The chiasm of masculine and feminine." Duquesne University. *Dissertation Abstracts*, vol. 33, no. 12, June 1973, p. 6974-A.

337a Walsh, Joseph. "Violence in Merleau-Ponty, Marx and Engels." Brandeis University, 1975.

338 Young, Marlene. "The political implications of phenomenological existentialism." Georgetown University. *Dissertation Abstracts*, vol. 34, no. 5, Nov. 1973, p. 2733-A.

339 Zeiler, M. Judith. "From contingency to hope: Merleau-Ponty's phenomenological philosophy in its impact upon his religious thought." Duquesne University, 1968.

INDIVIDUAL WORKS   53

SECTION THREE:

STUDIES OF INDIVIDUAL WORKS OF MERLEAU-PONTY

1) LA STRUCTURE DU COMPORTEMENT (1942)

340 Alquié, Ferdinand. "Etude sur le comportement." *Cahiers du Sud*, vol. 31, no. 267, août-septembre 1944, pp. 48-54.

341 Anonymous. "*La Structure du comportement.*" *Revue de Métaphysique et de Morale*, vol. 50, no. 4, octobre 1943, pp. 307-308. [a review]

342 Anonymous. "*The Structure of Behavior.*" *The Heytrop Journal*, vol. 8, 1967, pp. 74-76. [a review].

343 Chamonin, M. "*La Structure du comportement.*" *Fiches Bibliographiques*, novembre 1943, no. 5.

344 Collins, James. "Annual Review of Philosophy." *Cross Currents*, vol. 14, Fall 1964, pp. 460-462.

345 Cooper, F. B. K. "Hegelian elements in Merleau-Ponty's *Structure du comportement.*" *International Philosophical Quarterly*, vol. XV, no. 4, Dec. 1975.

346 Cuzin, François. "*La Structure du comportement.*" *Confluences*, tome 3, no. 19, 1943, pp. 460-463.

347 Galindez, J. "M. Merleau-Ponty, *La Estructura del comportamiento.*" *Humanitas*, vol. 7, 1959, pp. 226-228.

348 Gendlin, Eugene T. "*The Structure of Behavior.*" *The Modern Schoolman*, vol. 42, Nov. 1964, pp. 87-96.

349 Lapointe, François H. "The body-soul dialectic in Merleau-Ponty's *Structure of Behavior.*" *The Modern Schoolman*, vol. L, no. 3, March 1973, pp. 281-291.

350 Lauer, Quentin. "*The Structure of Behavior.*" *The New Scholasticism*, vol. XXXX, 1966, pp. 126-128.

351 Moloney, R. "*The Structure of Behavior.*" *The Heythrop Journal*, vol. VIII, 1967, pp. 74-76.

INDIVIDUAL WORKS

352   Pignanoli, S. "*La Struttura del comportamento.*"
        Humanitas (Brescia), vol. XIX, 1964, pp. 518-520.

353   Riverso, E. "*La Struttura del comportamento.*"
        Rassegna di Scienze Filosofiche, vol. XVI, 1963,
        pp. 369-371.

354   Rouart, Julien. "*La Structure du comportement* de
        Maurice Merleau-Ponty." *L'Evolution Psychiatrique*,
        1947, pp. 333-350.

355   Scotti, Giuseppina. "Originarietà e relazione in
        Merleau-Ponty." *Aut Aut*, vol. VII, no. 38, March
        1957, pp. 172-184.

356   Taylor, Charles. "Genesis." *New Statesman*, vol.
        LXX, no. 1799, Sept. 3, 1965, pp. 326-327.

357   Waelhens, Alphonse de. "Une philosophie de l'ambi-
        guïté," préface to the 2nd ed. of *La Structure
        du comportement*. Paris: Presses Universitaires
        de France, 1949.

358   Wild, John D. "Foreword" to *The Structure of Be-
        havior*. Translated by Alden Fisher. Boston:
        Beacon Press, 1963, pp. xii-xvii.

359   Wulff, E. "*La Structure du comportement.*" *Philo-
        sophisches Jahrbuch*, vol. LXIV, 1955, pp. 406-417.

2) LA PHENOMENOLOGIE DE LA PERCEPTION (1945)

360   Alquié, Ferdinand. "Une philosophie de l'ambiguïté:
        l'existentialisme de Maurice Merleau-Ponty."
        Fontaine, vol. XI, no. 59, avril 1947, pp. 47-70.

361   Anonymous. "*La Phénomenologie de la perception.*"
        Revue de Métaphysique et de Morale, vol. LI, no. 2,
        avril 1946, pp. 183-184.

362   Anonymous. "*The Phenomenology of Perception.*" *The
        Heythrop Journal*, vol. V, 1964, pp. 235-237.

363   Anonymous. "Phenomenology of Perception." *The Times
        Literary Supplement*, vol. XXXXV, 1945, pp. 106-107.

364   Anzieu, Didier. "Thèses et diplômes d'études
        supérieures de philosophie." *Essais et Etudes
        Universitaires*, 1946, pp. 115-121.

INDIVIDUAL WORKS 55

365 Ballard, Edward G. "The philosophy of Merleau-Ponty," pp. 165-187 in *Tulane Studies in Philosophy: Studies in Hegel*, vol. 9. The Hague: Martinus Nijhoff, 1960.

366 Ballard, Edward G. "On cognition of the pre-cognitive: Merleau-Ponty." *Philosophical Quarterly*, vol. XI, no. 44, July 1961, pp. 238-244.

367 Bastable, J. D. "M. Merleau-Ponty, *Phenomenology of Perception*." *Philosophical Studies* (Maynooth), vol. XII, 1963, pp. 320-321.

368 Beauvoir, Simone de. "*La Phénoménologie de la perception* de Maurice Merleau-Ponty." *Les Temps Modernes*, 1ère année, no. 2, novembre 1945, pp. 363-367.

Bertoldi, Eugene F. See Time (No. 1368).

Bertoldi, Eugene F. See Dissertation (No. 263).

369 Caillois, Roland. "Note sur l'analyse réflexive et la réflexion phénoménologique: à propos de la *Phénoménologie de la perception* de M. Merleau-Ponty." *Deucalion*, vol. I, 1946, pp. 125-139.

370 Caillois, Roland. "De la perception à l'histoire. La philosophie de Maurice Merleau-Ponty." *Deucalion*, vol. II, 1947, pp. 57-85.

371 Cardoletti, P. "*Fenomenologia della percezione*." *La Scuola Cattolica*, vol. LXXXXV, 1967, supl. bibl., pp. 78-80.

372 Carlini, Armando. "*Phenomenologie de la perception*." *Giornale Critico della Filosofia Italiana*, vol. XXVI, nos. 3-4, 1947, pp. 409-413.

373 Collins, James. "Annual Review of Philosophy." *Cross Currents*, vol. XIII, no. 2, 1963, pp. 197-198.

374 Cotten, Jean-Pierre. "Les lectures de Merleau-Ponty: À propos de la *Phénoménologie de la perception*. *Revue de Métaphysique et de Morale*, vol. LXXVII, no. 3, juillet-sept. 1972, pp. 307-328.

375 DeLattre, Alain. "L'univers de la perception et ses dimensions chez Maurice Merleau-Ponty." *Revue Philosophique de la France et de l'Etranger*, tome 164, juillet-septembre 1974, pp. 273-292.

INDIVIDUAL WORKS

376   Desanti, Jean-T. "Retour à Berkeley," pp. 107-124 in R. Garaudy et al. *Mésaventures de l'anti-marxisme. Les malheurs de M. Merleau-Ponty.* Paris: Editions Sociales, 1956.

Dreyfus, Hubert L. See Dissertation (No. 278).

377   Dreyfus, Hubert L., and Thodes, S. J. "The three worlds of Merleau-Ponty." *Philosophy and Phenomenological Research,* vol. XXII, no. 4, June 1962, pp. 559-565.

378   Dupré, Louis. "Phenomenology of Perception." *The New Scholasticism,* vol. XXXX, 1966, pp. 199-201.

379   Eckardt, A. "M. Merleau-Pontys *Phänomenologie der Wahrnehmung.*" *Philosophischer Literaturanzeiger,* vol. XIX, 1966, pp. 193-197.

380   Fisher, Alden L. "Phenomenology of Perception." *The Modern Schoolman,* vol. XXXXII, Nov. 1964, pp. 100-104.

381   Fontan, Pierre. "Le primat de l'acte sur l'énoncé. A propos de la *Phénoménologie de la perception.*" *Revue Philosophique de Louvain,* vol. LIII, no. 37, Feb. 1955, pp. 40-53.

382   Forest, André. "Chronique de philosophie." *Revue Thomiste,* vol. XXXXVI, 1946, pp. 405-406.

383   Gianne, W. J. "Phenomenology of Perception." *The Australian Journal of Philosophy,* vol. XXXXII, no. 1, May 1964, pp. 135-142.

384   Grenier, Jean. "La philosophie." *L'Arche,* vol. III, no. 10, octobre 1945, pp. 135-136.

385   Guillaume, Paul. "*Phénoménologie de la perception.*" *Journal de Psychologie Normale et Pathologique,* vol. XXXIX, 1946, pp. 489-494.

386   Gurwitsch, Aron. "Phenomenology of Perception." *Philosophical Review,* vol. LXXIII, July 1964, pp. 417-422.

387   Gurwitsch, Aron. "*Phénoménologie de la perception.*" *Philosophy and Phenomenological Research,* vol. X, no. 3, March 1950, pp. 442-445.

388   G. Y. "La *Phénoménologie de la perception.*" *Paru,* no. 14, Janvier 1946, pp. 99-101.

389   Haden, James C. "Books in the field: Philosophy." *Wilson Library Bulletin,* vol. XXXX, no. 2, Oct. 1965, pp. 422-431.

INDIVIDUAL WORKS 57

390   Hayen, André. "La phénoménologie de M. Merleau-Ponty et la métaphysique." *Revue Philosophique de Louvain*, vol. L, no. 25, Feb. 1952, pp. 102-123.

Hogemann, Friedrich. See Dissertation (No. 292a).

391   Jacques, J. H. "Exorcizing the ghost in the machine." *The Listener*, vol. LXXIV, no. 1893, July 8, 1965, pp. 49-51. [M.-P. and G. Ryle.]

392   Kaufmann, Fritz. "*Phénomenologie de la perception*." *Erasmus* vol. II, nos. 7-8, Jan. 15, 1959, columns 202-206.

393   Kaulbach, F. "Phänomenologie der Wahrnehmung, Merleau-Pontys." *Theologische Revue*, vol. LXIV, 1968, pp. 85-94.

394   Kockelmans, Joseph J. "Maurice Merleau-Ponty," pp. 349-355, in *Phenomenology*. Garden City, N. Y.: Anchor Books, Doubleday and Co., Inc. 1967.

395   Kullman, Michael, and Taylor, Charles. "The pre-objective world." *Review of Metaphysics*, vol. XII, no. 1, Sept. 1958, pp. 108-132. Reprinted in Maurice Natanson, ed., *Essays in Phenomenology*, pp. 116-136. The Hague: Martinus Nijhoff, 1966.

396   Kullman, Michael, and Taylor, Charles. "Reply to T. N. Munson." *Review of Metaphysics*, vol. XII, June 1959, pp. 624-632.

397   Kwant, Remy C. "Merleau-Ponty's phaenomenologie van de perceptie." *Wijsgerig Perspectief de Maatschappin en Wetenschap*, vol. II, 1961-1962, pp. 267-280.

Lapointe, François H. See Time (No. 1372).

398   Lauer, Quentin. "Phenomenology of Perception." *Thought*, vol. XXXIX, 1964, pp. 144-145.

Moreau, Joseph. See Books, French (No. 188).

399   Philippe, M. D. "Exposé de la phénoménologie de M. Merleau-Ponty." *Nova et Vetera*, 1951, pp. 132-146.

400   Philippe, M. D. "Réflexions sur la phénoménologie de M. Merleau-Ponty." *Nova et Vetera*, 1951, pp. 198-209.

INDIVIDUAL WORKS

401   Saffirio, Guido. "Introduzione e commenti," to Merleau-Ponty, *Esperienza e libertà*. Antologia della *Fenomenologia della percezione*. Traduzione di A. Bonomi. (Biblioteca di filosofia e pedagogia). Torino: G. B. Paravia, 1973, xxxii-152p.

402   Schmitt, Richard. "Maurice Merleau-Ponty." (two parts). *Review of Metaphysics*, vol. XIX, no. 3, March 1966, pp. 491-516; and *Ibid.*, vol. XIX, no. 4, June 1966, pp. 728-741.

403   Schulte, G. "Vomm Sinn der Wahrnehmung. Die Wissenschaltslehre Fichtes und Merleau-Pontys *Phänomenologie der Wahrnehmung*." *Tijdschrift voor Filosofie*, vol. XXXI, Dec. 1969, pp. 732-738.

404   Scotti, Giuseppina. "Originarietà e relazione in Merleau-Ponty." *Aut Aut*, vol. VII, no. 39, May 1957, pp. 295-309.

405   Scotti, Giuseppina. "Originalità e relazione nella *Phénoménologie de la perception*." *Aut Aut*, vol. VII, no. 41, Sept. 1957, pp. 436-442.

406   Scotti, Giuseppina. "Sulla percezione in Merleau-Ponty." *Aut Aut*, vol. VII, no. 42, Nov. 1957, pp. 512-523.

407   Semerari, Giuseppe. "Critica e projetto dell'uomo nella fenomenologia di Maurice Merleau-Ponty." *Il Pensiero*, vol. V, no. 3, Sept.-Dec. 1960, pp. 329-359.

408   Semerari, Giuseppe. "Esistenzialismo e marxismo nella *Fenomenologia della percezione*." *Rivista di Filosofia*, vol. LII, no. 3, July 1961, pp. 330-353.

410   Semerari, Giuseppe. "Scienza e filosofia nella *Fenomenologia della percezione*." *Aut Aut*, no. 66, Nov. 1961, pp. 481-497.

411   Spiegelberg, Herbert. "The phenomenological philosophy of Maurice Merleau-Ponty," pp. 516-560, vol. II, in *The Phenomenological Movement. A Historical Introduction*. The Hague: Martinus Nijhoff, 1960.

412   Tiliette, Xavier. "Le corps et le temps dans la *Phénoménologie de la perception*." *Studia Philosophica*, vol. XXIV, 1964, pp. 193-204.

       Tilliette, Xavier. See Book, French (No. 194).

INDIVIDUAL WORKS 59

413 Trogu, G. "Merleau-Ponty e la *Fenomenologia della percezione.*" *Il Pensiero Critico*, vol. II, no. 4, Oct.-Dec. 1960, pp. 16-65.

414 Trogu, G. "Osservazioni attorno a un passo della *Phénoménologie de la perception* di Merleau-Ponty." *Aut Aut*, vol. XXIV, 1964, pp. 193-204.

415 Urango, E. "Maurice Merleau-Ponty: fenomenologia y existencialismo." *Filosofia y Letras*, vol. XV, no. 30, 1948, pp. 219-242.

416 Vandenbussche, Franz. "Phänomenologie der Wahrnehmung." *Bijdragen*, vol. XXVII, 1966, pp. 565-566.

417 Virasoro, Manuel. "Merleau-Ponty y el mundo al nivel de la percepción." *Ciencia y Fé*, vol. XIII, 1957, pp. 147-153. Trans. by Michael Correa as "Merleau-Ponty and the world of perception." *Philosophy Today*, vol. III, no. 1, Spring 1959, pp. 66-72.

418 Waelhens, Alphonse de. "De la phénoménologie à l'existentialisme," in *Le Choix, le monde, l'existence*. (Cahiers du Collège Philosophique). Paris: Arthaud, 1947.

419 Waelhens, Alphonse de. "Phénoménologie et métaphysique." *Revue Philosophique de Louvain*, Aug. 1949, pp. 366-376.

420 Waelhens, Alphonse de. "Over de betekenis van het oeuvre Merleau-Ponty." *Tijdschrift voor Filosofie*, vol. XII, 1950, pp. 477-503.

421 Warnock, Mary. "Phenomenology of Perception." *The Philosophical Quarterly* (Scotland), vol. XIV, 1964, pp. 372-375.

422 Witté, A. de. "Phaenomenologie van de perceptie." *Algemeen Nederlands Tijdschrift voor Wijsbegeerte en Psychologie*, vol. XXXIX, no. 2, 1947, pp. 180-185.

423 Wulff, E. "Phénoménologie de la perception." *Philosophisches Jahrbuch*, vol. LXIV, 1955, pp. 406-417.

424 Yagüe, Joaquín. "M. Merleau-Ponty y la fenomenología." *Crisis*, vol. XVII, 1970, pp. 115-242.

60 INDIVIDUAL WORKS

3) <u>HUMANISME ET TERREUR</u> (1947)

      Albert, Hughes. See Dissertation (No. 258).

425   Anonymous. *"Humanisme et terreur." Revue Philosophique de la France et de l'Etranger*, vol. LXXIV, 1949, pp. 490-491.

426   Berl, Emmanuel. *De l'innocence. Etudes et essais.* Paris: R. Julliard, 1947.

427   Berl, Emmanuel. *A Contretemps.* Paris: Gallimard, 1969.

      Bien, Joseph. See Dissertation (No. 266).

428   Caillois, Roland. "Destin de l'humanisme marxiste: A propos de M. Merleau-Ponty, *Humanisme et terreur." Critique*, vol. IV, no. 22, mars 1948, pp. 243-251.

429   Caillois, Roland. "Le monde vécu et l'histoire," pp. 7-24, in *L'Homme, le monde, l'histoire.* Paris Arthaud, 1948.

430   Campbell, Robert. "Monsieur Merleau-Ponty et ses lecteurs." *Paru*, no. 37, decembre 1947, pp. 49-51

431   Cardoletti, P. "Umanesimo e terrore." *La Scuola Cattolica*, vol. LXXXVII, 1969, supl. bibl. pp. 140-141.

      Centineo, Ettore. See Book, Italian (No. 222).

432   Christianus (pseud.) "Sainte Antigone." *La Vie Intellectuelle*, vol. XV, no. 1, Janvier 1947, pp. 1-4.

433   Desanti, Jean T. "Merleau-Ponty et la décomposition de l'idéalisme." *La Nouvelle Critique*, vol. IV' no. 37, juin 1952, pp. 63-82.

434   Desgraupes, P. "Le phénomène Koestler." *Fontaine*, vol. XI, no. 59, avril 1947, pp. 112-130.

435   Edie, James M. *"Humanism and Terror." Journal of Value Inquiry*, vol. IV, 1970, pp. 314-320.

436   Estall, H. M. *"Humanism and Terror." Dialogue*, vol. VIII, no. 3, Dec. 1969, pp. 526-528.

INDIVIDUAL WORKS   61

Howard, Dick. See Books, English, Gillan (No. 135).

437   Kolakowski, Leozek, "Obsolete therefore instructive."
      The New York Review of Books, vol. XV, no. 4, Sept.
      3, 1970, pp. 23-25.

438   Kulenkampff, Arend. *"Humanismus und Terror." Die
      Neue Rundschau*, 1968, pp. 155-161.

439   Lefort, Claude. "La contradiction de Trotsky et le
      problème révolutionnaire." *Les Temps Modernes*,
      4e année, no. 39, 1949, pp. 23-36.

440   Lienert, Edmond. "Koestler et l'intelligence de
      gauche." *La République Moderne*, no. 27-28, 1947.

441   Martinet, Daniel D. "Les intellectuels et le goût du
      pouvoir." *La Révolution Prolétarienne*, no. 302,
      mai 1947, pp. 73-88.

442   Monnerot, Jules. "Liquidation et justification."
      La Nef, vol. IV, no. 27, fevrier 1947, pp. 8-19.

443   Monnerot, Jules. "Réponse aux *Temps Modernes*, 1."
      La Nef, vol. IV' no. 37, decembre 1947, pp. 32-44.

444   Monnerot, Jules. "Du mythe à l'obscurantisme.
      Réponse aux *Temps modernes*, II," *La Nef*, vol. V,
      no. 39, fevrier 1948, pp. 3-21.

445   O'Neill, John. "Introduction," to *Humanism and Ter-
      ror*. trans. by John O'Neill. Boston. Beacon
      Press, 1969.

446   Patri, Aimé. "Bibliographie du débat autour du livre
      de M. Merleau-Ponty, *Humanisme et terreur*."
      Paru, no. 37, decembre 1947, pp. 51-52.

447   Patri, Aimé. *"Humanisme et terreur." Paru*, no. 42,
      mai 1948, pp. 61-62.

448   Patri, Aimé. "La philosophie de la police politique."
      Masses, nos. 7-8, 1947, pp. 7-8.

449   Ricoeur, Paul. "Le yogi, le commissaire, le prolé-
      taire et le prophète." *Christianisme Social*,
      vol. LVII, 1949, pp. 150-157.

450   Ricoeur, Paul. "La pensée engagée. Maurice Merleau-
      Ponty." *Esprit*, vol. XVI, decembre 1948, pp. 911-
      916.

451   Somerville, John. "Violence, politics and morality."
      Philosophy and Phenomenological Research, vol.XXXII,
      Dec. 1971, pp. 241-249.

INDIVIDUAL WORKS

452 Spiegelberg, Herbert. "French existentialism: Its social philosophy." *Kenyon Review*, vol. XVI, no. 3, Summer 1954, pp. 446-462.

453 Weyembergh, Maurice. "Merleau-Ponty et Camus. *Humanisme et terreur et Ni victimes ni bourreaux.*" *Annales de l'Institut de Philosophie*, 1971, pp. 53-99.

4) SENS ET NON-SENS (1948)

454 Anonymous. "Sens et non-sens." *Bulletin Critique du Livre Francais*, vol. IV, 1949, p. 37.

455 Battaglini, A. "Senso e non-senso di Merleau-Ponty e l'estetica fenomenologica italiana." *Il Verri*, no. 10, 1963, pp. 85-97.

456 E. B. "Sens et non-sens." *Revue Philosophique de la France et de l'Etranger*, vol. LXXV, 1950, pp. 352-353.

457 Campbell, Robert. "Sens et non-sens." *Paru*, no. 51, fevrier-mars 1949, pp. 66-67.

458 Crastre, Victor. "Un tour d'horizon sur le monde: A propos de *Sens-et non-sens.*" *Critique*, vol. V, no. 36, may 1949, pp. 470-474.

459 Daly, James. "Sense and non-sense." *Philosophical Studies* (Maynooth), vol. XVI, 1967, pp. 317-319.

460 Delfgaauw, Bernardus. "Sens et non-sens." *Algemeen Nederlands Tijdschrift voor Wijsbegeerte Psychologie*, vol. XXXIII, 1950-1951, pp. 46-48.

461 Dreyfus, Hubert L. and Dreyfus, Patricia Allen. "Translators' Introduction" to *Sense and Non-Sense*. Evanston, Ill.: Northwestern University Press, 1964.

462 Fisher, Alden. "Sense and Non-Sense." *The Modern Schoolman*, vol. XXXVI, 1968, pp. 357-360.

463 Franco, G. "M. Merleau-Ponty, *Senso e non-senso.*" *Giornale Critico della Filosofia Italiana*, vol. XXXII, 1963, pp. 112-119.

464 Greiner, D. "Sense and Non-Sense." *Review of Existential Psychology and Psychiatry*, vol. V, 1965, pp. 198-199.

INDIVIDUAL WORKS 63

465 Havet, J. *"Sens et non-sens." Philosophy and Phenomenological Research*, vol. XI, 1950-1951, p. 236.

456 Tonini, Valerio. "*Senso e non-senso* di Merleau-Ponty." *La Fiera Letteraria*, vol. XVII, no. 35, Sept. 9, 1962, p. 1.

5) LES AVENTURES DE LA DIALECTIQUE (1955)

Albert, Hughes. See Dissertation (No. 258).

467 Anonymous. "Merleau-Ponty, *Les Aventures de la dialectique.*" *Philosophisches Jahrbuch*, vol. LXIV, 1956, pp. 437-438.

468 Aron, Raymond. "Aventures et mésaventures de la dialectique." *Preuves*, jan. 1956. Reprinted pp. 63-116 in *Marxismes imaginaires. D'une Sainte Famille à l'autre*. Paris: Gallimard, 1970. English trans. pp. 45-80 in *Marxism and the Existentialists*. New York: Harper & Row, 1969.

469 Aron, Raymond. "Le fanatisme, la prudence et la foi." *Preuves*, février 1956. Reprinted pp. 117-159 in *Marxismes imaginaires*. English trans. in *Marxism and the Existentialists*, pp. 81-108.

470 Aubenque, Pierre. "Dialectique et action: à propos des *Aventures de la dialectique* de M. Merleau-Ponty." *Recherches de Philosophie*: II, aspects de la dialectique. 1956, pp. 329-344.

471 Audry, Colette. "*Les aventures de la dialectique.*" *L'Express*, no. 105, mai 28, 1955, p. 13.

472 Bien, Joseph. "Translator's Introduction," pp. ix-xxix, *Adventures of the Dialectic*. Evanston, Ill.: Northwestern University Press, 1973.

473 Beauvoir, Simone de. "Merleau-Ponty et le pseudo-sartrisme." *Les Temps Modernes*, 10e année, nos. 114-115, juillet 1955, pp. 2072-2122. Reprinted in *Privilèges*, pp. 203-272. Paris: Gallimard, 1955.

474 Borne, Etienne. "*Les Aventures de la dialectique* de Maurice Merleau-Ponty." *La Vie Intellectuelle*, 26e année, no. 7, juillet 1955, pp. 6-14.

64   INDIVIDUAL WORKS

Caveing, Maurice. See Books, French, Garaudy, pp. 125-132 (No. 175).

475   Châtelet, François. "M. Merleau-Ponty et la dernière mode de l'anticommunisme." *La Nouvelle Critique,* vol. VII, no. 67, juillet-aout 1955, pp. 30-48.

Cogniot, Georges. See Books, French, Garaudy, pp. 149-157 (No. 175).

476   Cottier, M. "Chronique sur le marxisme." *Revue Thomiste*, vol. LIX, 1950, 1959, pp. 163-168.

Desanti, Jean-T. See Books, French, Garaudy, pp. 107-124 (No. 175).

477   Dufrenne, Mikel. "Les aventures de la dialectique ou les avatars d'une amitié philosophique." *Combat*, sept. 29, 1955. Reprinted pp. 169-173 in *Jalons*. The Hague: Martinus Nijhoff, 1966.

478   A.D. "*Les Aventures de la dialectique.*" *Philosophisches Jahrbuch,* vol. LXIV, 1955, pp. 437-438.

Garaudy, Roger, et al. See Books, French, Garaudy (No. 175).

479   Gisselbrecht, André. "Les aventures du 'marxisme occidental'." *La Nouvelle Critique*, vol. VII, no. 67, 1955, pp. 49-73.

480   Gisselbrecht, André. "Merleau-Ponty, la dialectique et la sociologie allemande." *La Nouvelle Critique*, vol. VII, no. 68, sept.-octobre 1955, pp. 33-57.

481   Golfin, C. "Chronique de philosophie politique." *Revue Thomiste*, vol. LVI, 1956, pp. 353-375.

482   Hamrick, William S. "Merleau-Ponty, *Adventures of the dialectic.*" *The Modern Schoolman*, vol. LII, no. 4, May 1975, pp. 455-458.

483   KAJ. See Communism.

484   Kanapa, Jean. "Théoriciens du désespoir." *La Nouvelle Critique*, vol. VII, no. 66, juin 1955, pp. 14-22.

Kanapa, Jean. See French Books, Garaudy, pp. 142-148 (No. 175).

485   Kopper, J. "*Les Aventures de la dialectique. Philosophischer Literaturanzeiger,*" vol. IX, 1956, pp. 66-71.

486   Kwant, Remy C. "De harmonische uitgroei van een wijsbegeerte. Naar aanleiding van de laatste publicatie van Maurice Merleau-Ponty." *Studia Catholica*, 1955, pp. 203-219.

487   Le Blond, Jean-Marie. "Le sens de l'histoire et l'action politique." *Etudes*, tome 287, novembre 1955, pp. 209-219.

488   Leduc, Victor. "Il n'y a pas de 'gauche' anticommuniste," pp. 133-141; see Books (No. 175).

489   Lefebvre, Henri. "M. Merleau-Ponty et la philosophie de l'ambiguïté." *La Pensée*, no. 68, juillet-août 1956, pp. 44-58; and *Ibid.*, no. 73, mai-juin 1957, pp. 37-52.

490   Lefebvre, Henri. "Les dilemmes de la dialectique." *Médiations*, no. 2, 1961, pp. 79-105.

Lefebvre, Henri. "Une philosophie de l'ambiguïté," pp. 99-106. See Books, French, Garaudy (No. 175).

491   Lukács, Georg. "Max Weber et la sociologie allemande." *La Nouvelle Critique*, vol. VII, no. 67, 1955, pp. 77-91.

Lukács, Georg. See pp. 158-160, in see Books, French, Garaudy (No. 175).

492   Mathieu, V. *"Les Aventures de la dialectique." Filosofia* (Torino), vol. IX, 1958, pp. 734-735.

493   *La Nouvelle Critique: Les Aventures de la dialectique.* Vol. VII, no. 67, juillet-août 1955. [Whole issue devoted to *Les Aventures de la dialectique.*] [Articles by Gisselbrecht (Nos. 479-480), Lefebvre, Garaudy, Lukacs (No. 496), and Châtelet (No. 475).]

O'Neill, John. See Books, English (No. 153).

494   O'Neill, John. *"Adventures of the Dialectic* (trans. by Joseph Bien)." *Dialogue*, vol. XIII, March 1974, pp. 220-222.

495   Pagani, M. *"Les Aventures de la dialectique." Rivista di Filosofia Neo-Scolastica,* vol. XXXXVII, 1955, pp. 676-679.

496   Patri, Aimé. "De l'opium des intellectuels à la cure de désintoxication." *Preuves*, vol. V, no. 53, juillet 1955, pp. 81-85.

INDIVIDUAL WORKS

Pauls, Arleen Laura. See Dissertation (No. 319).

497 Platen, A. von. "Les Aventures de la dialectique." *Archiv für Recht- und Sozialphilosophie* (Bern), Vol. XXXXII, 1956, pp. 86-97.

498 Quilliot, R. "De Nekrassov à Merleau-Ponty: misères de la philosophie et du journalisme." *Revue Socialiste*, no. 92, décembre 1955, pp. 551-555.

499 Sarano, J. "Les Aventures de la dialectique." *Les Etudes Philosophiques*, vol. X, 1955, pp. 752-754.

500 Sérant, Paul. "Maurice Merleau-Ponty et la pensée de gauche." *La Revue des deux Mondes*, 1er juillet 1955, pp. 117-127.

501 Sheridan, James F. "On ontology and politics: A polemic." *Dialogue*, vol. VII, no. 3, Dec. 1968, pp. 449-460.

502 Shiner, Larry. "A phenomenological approach to historical knowledge." *History and Theory*, vol. VIII, no. 2, 1969, pp. 260-274.

503 Siméon, J.-P. "Vérité et idéologie. La critique de la théorie des idéologies dans les premières oeuvres de Merleau-Ponty." *L'Arc*, no. 46, 1971, pp. 48-55.

504 Sorel, Jean-Jacques. "Merleau-Ponty contre Sartre." *France Observateur*, vol. VI, no. 263, 26 mai 1955, pp. 16-18.

505 Spurling, Laurie. "Adventures of the Dialectic." *Journal of the British Society for Phenomenology*, vol. VI, no. 1, Jan. 1975, pp. 63-65.

506 Strasser, Stephen. "Merleau-Ponty's bijdrage tot de sociaalfilosofie. Interpretatie en critiek." *Tijdschrift voor Filosofie*, vol. XXIX, 1967, pp. 427-470.

Surkim, Marvin L. See Dissertation (No. 332).

507 Ulmo, Jean. "Une étape de la pensée politique." *Critique*, vol. XI, no. 98, juillet 1955, pp. 625-643.

508 Valentini, Francesco. "Les Aventures de la dialectique." *Rassegna Critica della Filosofia*, vol. V, 1956, pp. 198-199.

509   Van Lier, Henri. "A propos de *Les Aventures de la dialectique:* philosophie et politique." *La Revue Nouvelle*, vol. XI, 1955, pp. 222-232.

510   Yanaishara, Isaku. "Situation of existentialism today." [In Japanese,] *Shiso*, vol. 381, 1956, pp. 17-26.

6) SIGNES (1960)

511   Alesanco, T. "M. Merleau-Ponty, *Signos*." *Augustinus*, vol. X, 1965, p. 263.

512   Anonymous. "Selecciones de libros." *Selecciones de Libros*, Dec. 1965.

513   Audry, Colette. *"Signes."* *L'Express*, no. 497, 22 décembre 1960.

514   A. G. "M. Merleau-Ponty, *Segni*." *Rivista di Filosofia Neo-Scolastica*, vol. LIX, 1967, pp. 652-653.

515   Cardoletti, P. *"Segni."* *La Scuola Cattolica*, vol. LXXXVII, 1969, pp. 141-142.

516   Debray, Régis. "Avec *Signes* Merleau-Ponty veut faire parler l'histoire." *Arts*, no. 802, 28 décembre 1960-3 janvier 1961, p. 3.

517   Deguy, Michel. "A propos de *Signes*." *La Nouvelle Revue Française*, vol. IX, no. 99, 1961, pp. 481-485.

518   Fernandez, Valeriano Bozal. "Maurice Merleau-Ponty: *Signes*." *Cuadernos Hispanoamericanos*, no. 191, Nov. 1965, pp. 414-416.

519   Fisher, Alden. *"Signs."* *The Modern Schoolman*, vol. XXXXVI, 1968, pp. 357-360.

520   Fragata, Julio. *"Sinais."* *Revista Portuguesa de Filosofia*, vol. XIX, 1963, pp. 205-206.

521   Greiner, D. *"Signs."* *Review of Existential Psychology and Psychiatry*, vol. V, 1965, pp. 113-116.

522   Hodges, Clark. *"Signs."* *Philosophy and Phenomenological Research*, vol. XXVI, no. 2, Dec. 1965, pp. 271-274.

68 INDIVIDUAL WORKS

523   Jacob, André. "M. Merleau-Ponty, *Signes*." *Les Etudes Philosophiques*, vol. XVI, 1961, pp. 264-265.

524   Jouhet, Serge. "Maurice Merleau-Ponty: *Signes*." *La Table Ronde*, no. 160, avril 1961, pp. 148-162.

525   Leganeta, F. "*Signos*." *Verdad y Vida*, vol. XXIII, 1965, pp. 723-724.

526   McCleary, Richard Calverton. "Translator's Preface," pp. ix-xxxii, to *Signs*. Evanston, Ill.: Northwestern University Press, 1964.

527   Nota, J. "*Signes*." *Bijdragen*, vol. XXV, 1964, p. 107.

528   Pariente, Jean-Claude. "Lecture de Merleau-Ponty." *Critique*, no. 186, novembre 1962, pp. 957-974; and *Ibid.*, no. 187, décembre 1962, pp. 1067-1078.

529   Piguet, Jean-Claude. "M. Merleau-Ponty, *Signes*." *Revue de Théologie et de Philosophie*, vol. XI, 1961, p. 206-207.

530   Riefstahl, H. "*Signes*." *Philosophischer Literaturanzeiger*, vol. XV, 1962, pp. 165-166.

531   Robberechts, L. "M. Merleau-Ponty, *Signes*." *La Revue Nouvelle*, vol. XXXV, 1962, p. 110.

532   Sokolowski, R. "*Signs*." *The New Scholasticism*, vol. XXXX, April 1966, pp. 246-250.

533   Taylor, Charles. "*Signs*." *The Philosophical Review*, vol. LXXVI, no. 1, Jan. 1967, pp. 113-117.

534   Turiel, B. "*Signos*." *Studium*, vol. V, 1965, pp. 605-606.

535   Valentini, Francesco. "*Signes*." *De Homine*, vol. I, 1962, pp. 232-233.

536   Waldenfels, Bernhard. "Merleau-Ponty, *Signes*." *Philosophsche Rundschau*, vol. XII, 1964, pp. 41-48.

7) L'OEIL ET L'ESPRIT

537   Arndt, H. W. Foreword to *Das Augen und der Geist. Philosophische Essays*. Hamburg: Rowohlt, 1967.

538   Invitto, Giovanni. "Introduzione" to *L'occhio e lo spirito*. Traduzione, introduzione e note a cura di Giovanni Invitto (Filosofi e pedagogisti). Lecce: Milella, 1971. 82p.

539   Kaufmann, Pierre. "De la vision picturale au désir de peindre." *Critique*, no. 211, décembre 1964, pp. 1047-1064.

540   Klein, Robert. "Peinture moderne et phénoménologie: à propos de *L'Oeil et l'esprit*." *Critique*, no. 191, avril 1963, pp. 336-348.

541   Kulenkampff, Arend. "Maurice Merleau-Ponty: Das Auge und der Geist." *Die Neue Rundschau*, 1968, pp. 155-161.

Kwant, Remy C. See Books, English, *From Phenomenology to metaphysics* (No. 142).

542   Pariente, Jean-Claude. "Lecture de Merleau-Ponty." *Critique*, no. 186, novembre 1962, pp. 957-974; and *Ibid*., no. 187, décembre 1962, pp. 1067-1078.

543   Sturani, Enrico. "M. Merleau-Ponty, *L'Oeil et l'esprit*." *Rivista di Filosofia*, vol. LVII, 1966, pp. 71-76.

544   Tilliette, Xavier. "*L'Oeil et l'esprit*." *Etudes*, tome 321, juillet, 1964, pp. 144-147.

545   Waelhens, Alphonse de. "Merleau-Ponty philosophe de la peinture." *Revue de Métaphysique et de Morale*, vol. LXVII, no. 4, octobre-décembre 1962, pp. 431-449.

8) LE VISIBLE ET L'INVISIBLE (1964)

546   Bannan, John F. "The 'later' thought of Merleau-Ponty." *Dialogue*, vol. V, no. 3, Dec. 1966, pp. 383-403.

547   Boehm, R. "Chaisma. Merleau-Ponty und Heidegger," pp. 369-393 in *Durchblicke: Martin Heidegger zum 80. Geburtstag*. Frankfurt am Main: Vittorio Klostermann, 1970.

548   Deguy, Michel. "*Le Visible et l'invisible*." *La Nouvelle Revue Française*, vol. XII, no. 138, juin 1964, pp. 1062-1072.

INDIVIDUAL WORKS

549   Derossi, Giorgio. "Dalla percezione alla visione: L'ontologia negativa dell'ultimo Merleau-Ponty." *Filosofia*, vol. XVI, 1965, pp. 333-357.

550   Espada, A. "M. Merleau-Ponty, *Lo Visible y lo invisible*." *Estudio Agustiniano*, vol. V, 1970, pp. 756-757.

551   Farrell Krell, David. "Maurice Merleau-Ponty on *Eros* and *Logos*." *Man and World*, vol. VII, no. 1, Feb. 1974, pp. 37-52.

552   Faye, Jean-Pierre. "Interphones et entrelacs." *Tel Quel*, no. 20, hiver 1965, pp. 84-90.

553   Flak, B. "*The Visible and the Invisible*." *Philosophic Quarterly*, vol. XX, July 1970, pp. 278-279.

554   Gauchet, Marcel. "Le lieu de la pensée." *L'Arc*, no. 46, 1971, pp. 19-30.

Gillespie, M. L. See Dissertation (No. 289).

555   Greppi, Alessandra. "*Le Visible et l'invisible* di M. Merleau-Ponty." *Rivista Filosofica Neo-Scolastica*, vol. LIX, March-April 1967, pp. 238-244.

556   Jacob, André. "M. Merleau-Ponty, *Le Visible et l'invisible*." *Les Etudes Philosophiques*, vol. XIX, 1964, pp. 469-470.

Joseph, Audrey Benderman. See Dissertation (No. 299).

557   Kaplan, F. "Maurice Merleau-Ponty: *Le Visible et l'invisible*." *Revue Philosophique de la France et de l'Etranger*, CLXI, no. 4, octobre-décembre 1971, pp. 497-504.

558   Kirkland, Jr., John D. "*The Visible and the Invisible*." *Philosophic Forum* (Dekalb), vol. IX, June 1971, pp. 372-374.

Kaufmann, Pierre. See *L'Oeil et l'esprit* (No. 539).

Kwant, Remy C. See Books English *From Phenomenology to Metaphysics* (No. 142).

559   Kwant, Remy C. "Merleau-Ponty's *Le Visible et l'invisible*." *Tijdschrift voor Filosofie*, vol. XXVI, 1964, pp. 627-629.

INDIVIDUAL WORKS 71

560   Lagueux, Maurice. "*Le Visible et l'invisible*. Par Maurice Merleau-Ponty." *Dialogue*, vol. V, no. 3, Dec. 1966, pp. 443-446.

561   Lapointe, François H. "The 'phenomenal' body in the later writings of Merleau-Ponty." *Journal of General Psychology*, vol. LXXXIV, April 1971, pp. 251-265.

562   Lefort, Claude, "L,idée 'd'être brut' et d''esprit sauvage'." *Les Temps Modernes*, 17e année, nos. 184-185, octobre-novembre 1961, pp. 256-286 [special commemorative issue].

563   Lefort, Claude. "Avertissement," pp. 9-14, and "Postface," pp. 337-360 in *Le Visible et l'invisible*. Paris: Gallimard, 1964.

564   Lingis, Alphonso. "Being in the interrogative Mood," pp. 78-91. See Books, English Gillan.

565   Lingis, Alphonso. "Translator's Preface," pp. XL-LVI, *The Visible and the Invisible*. Evanston, Ill.: Northwestern University Press, 1968.

566   Montagnes, B. "Merleau-Ponty, *Le Visible et l'invisible*." *Revue des Sciences Philosophiques et Théologiques*, vol. 49, 1965, pp. 109-110.

567   Montull, Tomas. "*Le Visible et l'invisible*." *Estudios Filosóficos*, vol. XIV, 1965, pp. 413-415.

568   M.A.S.G. "*Le Visible et l'invisible*." *Cuadernos Urugyayos de Filosofía*, vol. III, 1964, pp. 304-308.

569   O'Malley, John. "*The Visible and the Invisible*." *Human Context, Le Domaine Humain*, vol. V, Nov. 1971, pp. 647-657.

570   Passeri Pignoni, V. "*Il Visible e il invisible*." *Incontri Culturali* (Roma), 1970, pp. 228-229.

571   Pontalis, J.-B. "Présence, entre les signes, absence." *L'Arc*, no. 46, 1971, pp. 56-66.

572   P. P. "Merleau-Ponty, *Le Visible et l'invisible*." *Giornale Critico della Filosofia Italiana*, vol. XXXXIII, 1964, pp. 621-622.

573   Saffirio, Guido. "*Il Visible e il invisible*." *Filosofia*, vol. XXI, 1970, pp. 268-274.

72 INDIVIDUAL WORKS

574   Schilardi de Barcena, Maria. "Merleau-Ponty: la
         fenomenologia en su ultima obra." *Philosophia*.
         Instituto de Filosofia de la Universidad Nacional
         de Cuyo, Mendoza, no. 37, 1971, pp. 111-124.

575   Simon, Gérard. *"Le Visible et l'invisible." Les
         Lettres Françaises*, vol. VI, no. 1032, 4-10 juin
         1964, p. 6; *Ibid.*, no. 1033, 11-17 juin 1964, p.
         6; *Ibid.*, no. 1034, 18-24 juin 1964, p. 6.

576   Sturani, Enrico. "Maurice Merleau-Ponty, *Le Visible
         et l'invisible.*" *Rivista di Filosofia*, vol. LVII,
         1966, pp. 71-76.

577   Taylor, Darrell. "On the making of man." *Review of
         Existential Psychology and Psychiatry*, vol. IX,
         nos. 2-3, Fall-Winter 1969, pp. 188-194.

578   Tilliette, Xavier. *"Le Visible et l'invisible."
         Etudes*, tome 321, 1964, p. 144.

579   Vander Gucht, R. *"Le Visible et l'invisible." La
         Revue Nouvelle*, vol. 41, 1965, p. 439.

         Waelhens, Alphonse de. See *L'Oeil et l'esprit*
         (No. 545).

580   Warnock, Mary. "Down (again) with Descartes." *New
         Society*, vol. V, no. 140, June 3, 1965, pp. 30-31.

           9) ELOGE DE LA PHILOSOPHIE (1953)

581   Callois, Roland. "L'ambiguïté de l'histoire et la
         certitude de la philosophie." *Critique*, vol. IX,
         no. 77, octobre 1953, pp. 867-874.

582   Collins, James. "Annual review of philosophy."
         Cross Currents, vol. XIV, Fall 1964, pp. 460-464.

583   Composita, D. *"Eloge de la philosophie." Salesianum*
         vol. XX, 1958, pp. 488-489.

584   Daly, James. "In Praise of Philosophy." *Philosophical Studies* (Maynooth), vol. XVI, 1967, pp. 317-319.

585   Delfgaauw, Bernardus. "De inaugurale rede van Maurice
         Merleau-Ponty." *Studia Catholica*, vol. XXVIII,
         1953, pp. 137-139.

INDIVIDUAL WORKS 73

586   Ecole, Jean. "Rentrée au Collège de France avec M. Merleau-Ponty." *Revue Thomiste*, tome 53, 1953, pp. 193-196.

587   Fragata, Julio. "M. Merleau-Ponty, *Elogio de la Filosofia.*" *Revista Portuguesa de Filosofia*, vol. XIX, 1963, p. 93.

588   Gianne, W. J. *"In Praise of Philosophy."* *The Australian Journal of Philosophy*, vol. 42, no. 1, May 1964, pp. 135-142.

589   Lauer, Quentin. *"In Praise of Philosophy."* *Thought*, vol. XXXIX, 1964, pp. 144-145.

590   Le Blond, Jean-Marie. "L'humanisme athée au Collège de France." *Etudes*, tome 276, mars 1953, pp. 326-341.

591   Mathieu, V. *"Elogio della filosofia."* *Filosofia* (Torino), vol. IX, 1958, pp. 734-735.

592   Millet, Louis. "Sur la leçon inaugurale de Maurice Merleau-Ponty dans la Chaire de Bergson au Collège de France." *Les Etudes Bergsoniennes*, vol. IV, 1956, pp. 230-236.

593   Noguez, L. *"Eloge de la philosophie."* *Divus Thomas*, vol. 58, 1955, pp. 215-216.

594   Paci, Enzo. "Introduzione" to *Elogio della Filosofia*. Torino: Paravia, 1958.

595   Pagani, M. *"Eloge de la philosophie."* *Rivista di Filosofia Neo-Scolastica*, vol. 46, 1954, pp. 398-401.

596   Plinval, Georges de. "Quand la vérité passe à travers Merleau-Ponty." *Ecrits de Paris*, février 1953, pp. 37-44.

597   Robinson, S. D. "M. Merleau-Ponty, *In Praise of Philosophy.*" *Philosophy and Phenomenological Research*, vol. XXV, 1964, p. 151.

598   Tollenaere, Maurice de. "Merleau-Ponty, *Lof der wijsbegeerte.*" *Streven*, vol. XXI, 1968, p. 717.

599   Truc, Gonzague. "L'existentialisme au Collège de France." *Hommes et Mondes*, 8e année, février 1953, pp. 172-177.

600   Valentini, Francesco. *"Eloge de la philosophie."* *Rassegna Critica della Filosofia*, vol. II, 1953, pp. 389-390.

74   INDIVIDUAL WORKS

601   Van Marter, Leslie E. "*In Praise of Philosophy.*"
        Ethics, vol. 77, no. 2, January 1967, pp. 154-158.

602   Zuchi, H. "Merleau-Ponty, *Eloge de la philosophie.*"
        Notas y Estudios de Filosofía, vol. V, no. 17,
        1954, pp. 37-38.

10) LRS RELATIONS DE L'ENFANT AVEC AUTRUI

603   Fileasi, Paolo. "Introduzione" a *Il Bambino e gli
        altri*. Trad. G. Goela. Roma: A. Armando, 1968.

11) RESUMES DE COURS au Collège de France 1952-1960 (1968)

604   Anonymous. "Surprise in the syllabus." *Times Literary Supplement*, no. 3501, April 3, 1969, p. 344.

605   Fukada, S. "*Résumés de cours au Collège de France
        1952-1960.*" *Bigaru*, vol. XXI, March 1971, pp.
        52-62.

606   Madison, Gary B. "*Résumés de cours*, by Maurice Merleau-Ponty. *Themes from the Lectures at the
        College de France 1952-1960.*" *Journal of the
        British Society for Phenomenology*, vol. III, no.
        3, Oct. 1972, pp. 295-297.

607   O'Neill, John. "Translator's Preface," pp. xi-xvii,
        in *Themes from the Lectures at the College de
        France 1952-1960*. Evanston, Ill.: Northwestern
        University Press, 1970.

12) L'UNION DE L'AME ET DU CORPS CHEZ MALEBRANCHE, BIRAN ET BERGSON (1968)

        Anonymous. See *Résumés Times Lit. Sup.*, (No. 604)

608   Armogathe, J.-R. "*L'Union de l'âme et du corps chez
        Malebranche, Maine de Biran et Bergson*, de M.
        Merleau-Ponty." *Revue Philosophique de Louvain*,
        vol. LXVII, 1969, pp. 497-500.

609   Deprun, Jean. "Introduction" à *L'Union de l'âme et
        du corps chez Malebranche, Biran et Bergson*.
        Paris: J. Vrin, 1968.

13) LA PROSE DU MONDE (1969)

610 Anonymous. "Expressing ourselves." *Times Literary Supplement*, no. 3541, Jan. 8, 1970, p. 36.

611 Fabre-Luce, Anne. "Le devenir des signes." *La Quinzaine Littéraire*, no. 85, 15-31 décembre 1969, pp. 22-24.

612 Foucault, Michel. "The prose of the world." *Diogènes*, no. 53, Spring 1966, pp. 17-37.

613 Jacobson, Paul. "One more new botched beginning: A review of *La Prose du monde*." *Research in Phenomenology*, vol. II, 1972, pp. 143-153.

614 Jannoud, Claude. "Merleau-Ponty linguiste." *Le Figaro Littéraire*, no. 1228, 1-7 decembre, 1969, pp. 23-24.

615 Lefort, Claude. "Introduction" to *La Prose du monde*. Paris: Gallimard, 1969.

616 Lingus, Alphonso. "Maurice Merleau-Ponty, *La Prose du monde*." *Man and World*, vol. III, nos. 3-4, Sept.-Nov. 1970, pp. 406-414.

617 Maiorana, M. T. "Un ouvrage posthume de Merleau-Ponty." *Revue de Synthèse*, tome XCII, 1971, pp. 321-323.

618 Montpetit, Raymond. "*La Prose du monde*. Par M. Merleau-Ponty." *Dialogue*, vol. IX, no. 3, Dec. 1970, pp. 502-505.

619 O'Neill, John. "Language and embodiment: an afterword." [*Tri-Quarterly*, no. 20, Winter 1971, pp. 29-32.] *The Prose of the World*, trans. by John O'Neill, Ibid., pp. 9-28.

620 Penco, Carlo. "*La Prose del monde* de Merleau-Ponty." *Rivista Filosofia Neo-Scolastica*, vol. LXV, April-June 1973, pp. 377-381.

621 Tilliette, Xavier. "La Prose du monde." *Etudes*, tome 332, Avril 1970, pp. 632-633.

14) THE PRIMACY OF PERCEPTION AND OTHER ESSAYS (1964)

622 Carr, David. "*The Primacy of Perception*." *Journal of Existentialism*, vol. VI, 1965-1966, pp. 116-126.

INDIVIDUAL WORKS

623 Edie, James M. "Introduction," to *The Primacy of Perception and other Essays on Phenomenological Psychology, the philosophy of art, history and politics.* Edited by James M. Edie. Evanston, Ill.: Northwestern University Press, 1964.

624 Fisher, Alden. "The Primacy of Perception." *The Modern Schoolman*, vol. XXXXVI, 1968, pp. 357-360.

625 Greiner, D. "The Primacy of Perception." *Review of Existential Psychology and Psychiatry*, vol. V, 1965, pp. 109-112.

626 Hodges, Clark. "The Primacy of Perception." *Philosophy and Phenomenological Research*, vol. XXVI, no. 2, Dec. 1965, pp. 271-274.

627 Taylor, Charles. "The Primacy of Perception." *The Philosophical Review*, vol. LXXVI, no. 1, Jan. 1967, pp. 113-117.

628 Lahey, John L. "The Primacy of Perception." *Dianoia* (Mexico), Spring 1970, pp. 1-12.

15) CONSCIOUSNESS AND THE ACQUISITION OF LANGUAGE (trans. 1973)

629 A. G. "*Consciousness and the Acquisition of language.* M. Merleau-Ponty." *Review of Metaphysics*, vol. XXVIII, no. 4, issue 112, June 1975, pp. 760-761.

16) THE ESSENTIAL WRITINGS OF MERLEAU-PONTY (1969) (ed. by Alden L. Fisher)

630 Kelbley, Charles A. "Notes on the essential Merleau-Ponty." *The Modern Schoolman*, vol. 48, no. 2, Jan. 1971, pp. 166-170.

GENERAL DISCUSSION 77

SECTION FOUR:

GENERAL DISCUSSION OF THE WORKS OF MERLEAU-PONTY

631   Alquié, Ferdinand. *La Nostalgie de l'être*. Paris: Presses Universitaires de France, 1955.

632   Anonymous. "Merleau-Ponty, fenomenologo existencialista." *Filosofia*, 1958, pp. 291-293.

633   Anonymous. "Lettres-arts-spectacles." *La Nouvel Observateur*, n.s., no. 4, 10 decembre 1964, pp. 30-31.

634   Antuñes, M. "Significação de Maurice Merleau-Ponty." *Brotéria* (Lisbon), vol. LXXIV, no. 5, 1962, pp. 546-560.

635   *Aristotelian Society (The). Supplementary* vol. XXXVII, 1963. Published for the Aristotelian Society by Harrison & Sons, 1963.

536   *Aut Aut*. Special issue devoted to Merleau-Ponty, no. 66, Nov. 1961, pp. 481-576.

537   Bakker, Reinout. "Maurice Merleau-Ponty," pp. 125-138 in *Filosofen van de 20e eeuw*. Onder redactie van C. P. Bertels en E. Petersma. Assen, Amsterdam, Van Gorcum: Amsterdam, Brussel, Intermediair, 1972.

638   Bannan, John F. "Merleau-Ponty mismanaged." *Journal of Existentialism*, vol. VII, Summer 1967, pp. 459-476. [See Schmitt, Phenomenology of Perception, no. 402.]

639   Beerling, R. F. "Maurice Merleau-Ponty." *De Gids. Algemeen Cultureel Maandblad*, vol. 76, no. 5, Supplement 1963, pp. 391-407.

640   Bense, M. "Über Merleau-Ponty." *Merkur*, vol. VI, no. 9, Sept. 1952, pp. 888-891.

641   Bergeron, André. "La conscience engagée dans le régime des significations selon Merleau-Ponty." *Dialogue*, vol. V, no. 2, Dec. 1966, pp. 373-382.

641a   Blackman, H. H. (ed.) *Reality, Man and Existence*. New York: Bantam Books, 1965.

642   Burnier, Michel-Antoine. "Actualité de Merleau-Ponty." *Le Magazine Littéraire*, no. 35, décembre 1969, pp. 35-37.

GENERAL DISCUSSION

643   Campbell, Robert. "De l'ambiguité à l'héroisme chez Merleau-Ponty." *Cahiers du Sud*, nos. 390-391, octobre-décembre 1966, pp. 273-284.

644   Carlini, Armando. "Filosofia dell'ambiguità e ambiguità della filosofia." *Giornale di Metafisica*, vol. V, 1957, pp. 541-554.

645   Carr, David. "Maurice Merleau-Ponty: Incarnate consciousness," pp. 369-429, in George A. Schrader, (ed.), *Existential Philosophers: Kierkegaard to Merleau-Ponty*. New York: McGraw-Hill, 1967.

646   Cascales, Charles. "M. Merleau-Ponty philosophe de l'engagement." *Convivium*, nos. 11-12, 1961, pp. 45-74.

647   Chaix-Ruy, J. "Une Philosophie de l,ambigüité, M. Merleau-Ponty." in *Les Grands courants de la pensée mondiale contemporaine*. I, 1, B. M. F. Sciacca, ed. Milano: C. Marzorati, 1958.

648   *Currents of Thought in French Literature. Essays in Memory of G. T. Clapton*. Oxford: Basil Blackwell, 1965; New York: Barnes & Noble, 1965. 370p.

649   Cuvillier, Armand. *Anthologie des philosophes français contemporains*. 2nd. rev. ed. Paris: Presses Universitaires de France, 1965. 209p.

650   Davy, M. M. "La philosophie contemporaine." *Synthèses*, vol. III, no. 7, 1948, pp. 34-43; *Ibid.*, no. 8, 1949, pp. 230-240; *Ibid.*, no. 10, 1949, pp. 105-111.

651   Desanti, Jean-T. "Merleau-Ponty et la décomposition de l'idéalisme." *La Nouvelle Critique*, vol. IV, no. 37, juin 1952, pp. 63-82.

652   Dubreuil, L. "Du développement de la philosophie du moi et d'un véritable existentialisme." *Revue de Métaphysique et de Morale*, vol. LXX, 1965, pp. 363-374.

653   Dufrenne, Mikel. *La Notion d'a priori*. Paris: Presses Universitaires de France, 1959. English trans.

654   Dufrenne, Mikel. "Maurice Merleau-Ponty." *Les Etudes Philosophiques*, vol. XVII, no. 1, janvier-mars 1962, pp. 81-92. Reprinted in *Jalons*, pp. 208-221. The Hague: Martinus Nijhoff, 1966.

655   Duméry, Henry. "La Philosophie du comportement, d'après Maurice Merleau-Ponty," pp. 185-187 in *Regards sur la philosophie contemporaine*. Paris: Casterman, 1956.

656   Earle, William. "Man as the impossibility of God," pp. 82-112 in *Christianity and Existentialism*. Evanston, Ill.: Northwestern University Press, 1963.

657   Edwards, Paul. *The Encyclopedia of Philosophy*, vol. V, pp. 279-282. New York: The Macmillan Co. & The Free Press, 1967.

658   Egebak, Niels. "Merleau-Ponty," pp. 92-111, in *Indskrifter" Essays om foenomenologi og aestetik*. Fredensborg: Arena, 1967.

659   Eubé, Charles. "Humanités d'aujourd'hui: ce qui est en nous." *Poésie 46*, vol. VII, no. 35, octobre-novembre 1946, pp. 129-133.

660   P. E. "Dictionnaire critique." *Ecrits de Paris*, no. 214, mai 1962, pp. 65-71.

661   Ferrater Mora, J. "M. Merleau-Ponty," pp. 179-180 in *Diccionario de Filosofia, 2*. Buenos Aires: Ed. Sudamericana, 1965, (5.a).

662   Fisher, Alden L. "Introduction," pp. 3-13, *The Essential Writings of Merleau-Ponty*, New York: Harcourt, Brace and World, 1969.

663   Fragata, Julio. "A filosofia de Merleau-Ponty." *Revista Portuguesa de Filosofia*, vol. XIX, April-June 1963, pp. 113-141.

664   *Französische Kultur 1962*. Köln: Verlag der Dokumente, 1962. 112p.

665   Garaudy, Roger. *Perspectives de l'homme. Existentialisme, pensée catholique, marxisme*. Paris: Presses Universitaires de France, 1960, 2nd ed. rev and corrected.

666   Holz, Hans Heinz. "Situierung eines Denkers. Bemerkungen zu Maurice Merleau-Ponty," pp. 317-329 in *Festschrift zum achtzigsten Geburtstag von Georg Lukács*, hrsg. von Frank Benseler. Neuwied-Berlin: Luchterhand, 1966.

666a   Hughes, H. Stuart. *The Obstructed Path: French Social Thought in the Years of Desperation, 1930-1960*. New York: Harper & Row, 1968.

GENERAL DISCUSSION

667 Ihde, Don. *Sense and Significance.* [pp. 123-127, 163-170, 175-179, and passim] (Duquesne Studies, Philosophy series no. 31). Pittsburgh: Duquesne University Press, 1973, distributed by Humanities Press, New York.

668 *Intériorité et vie spirituelle. Recherces et débats* du Centre catholique des intellectuels français, nouv. série, cahier no. 7, avril 1964.

669 Jolivet, Jean. "Chroniques philosophiques." *Recherches et Débats*, no. 45, décembre 1963, pp. 169-182.

670 Kockelmans, Joseph J. "Maurice Merleau-Ponty," pp. 349-355 in Joseph J. Kockelmans, ed., *Phenomenology.* Garden City: Doubleday, Anchor Books, 1967.

671 Kwant, Remy C. "Maurice Merleau-Ponty: de hoop en de wereld." *Kultuurleven*, vol. XXIII, 1956, pp. 137-145.

672 Kwant, Remy C. "De zingedachte van Maurice Merleau-Ponty." *Bijdragen der Philosophie en Theologie*, 1955, pp. 1-31 [Summary in French]

673 Kwant, Remy C. "De geslotenheid van Merleau-Ponty's wijsbegeerte." *Tijdschrift voor Filosofie*, vol. XIX, 1957, pp. 217-271. [Summary in French]

674 Kwant, Remy C. "De wijsbegeerte van Merleau-Ponty." *Algemeen Nederlands Tijdschrift voor Wijsbegeerte en Psychologie*, vol. LIV, 1961-1962, pp. 1-21.

675 Lacan, Jacques. "Maurice Merleau-Ponty." *Les Temps Modernes*, 17e année, nos. 184-185, octobre-novembre 1961, pp. 245-254 [Special commemorative issue]

676 Lacroix, Jean. "Un philosophe de l'ambiguité: Maurice Merleau-Ponty," pp. 140-174, in *Panorama de la philosophie française contemporaine*, edited by Jean Lacroix. Paris: Presses Universitaires de France, 1966. [2nd rev ed. 1968, pp. 137-144]

677 Laporte, Roger. "Merleau-Ponty," in *Quinze variations sur un thème biographique.* (Coll. "Textes"). Paris: Flammarion, 1975.

677a Lee, Edward N. and Mandelbaum, Maurice (eds.) *Phenomenology and Existentialism.* Baltimore: The Johns Hopkins Press, 1967. [chapter by F. A. Olafson, pp. 179-206]

678   Lefebvre, Henri. "M. Merleau-Ponty et la philosophie de l'ambiguité." *La Pensée*, no. 68, juillet-août 1956, pp. 44-58; *Ibid.* no. 73, mai-juin 1957, pp. 37-52.

679   Lefort, Claude. "De la réponse à la question." *Les Temps Modernes*, 9e année, no. 101, février 1954, pp. 157-184.

680   Lefort, Claude. "Etude: Merleau-Ponty--Une pensée au-delà de la pensée." *Le Monde* [*des Livres*], no. 7857, 18 avril 1970, pp. 4-5.

681   Lefort, Claude. "Maurice Merleau-Ponty," pp. 206-214 in *Contemporary Philosophy, III. A survey*. Edited by Raymond Klibansky. Metaphysics, phenomenology, language, and structure. Firenze: La Nuova Italia, 1969.

682   Llavona, Rafael. "Merleau-Ponty a los diez años de su muerte. Ensayo bibliografico." *Pensamiento* (Madrid), vol. XXVII, 1971, pp. 255-307.

683   Lobet, Marcel. "La vie littéraire." *Revue Générale Belge*, 90e année, 15 février 1954, pp. 709-715.

684   Lyotard, Jean-François. *Discours figure*. Paris: Klincksieck, 1971.

685   Macksey, Richard, ed. *Velocities of Change. Critical Essays from Modern Language Notes*. Baltimore: Johns Hopkins Press, 1973.

686   Maione, Pasquale. "La dimensione archeologica dell'uomo. (L'urdoxa di M. Merleau-Ponty.)" *Rassegna di Scienze Filosofiche*, vol. I, no. 22, 1969, pp. 255-266.

687   Malverne, L. *Signification de l'homme*. Paris: Presses Universitaires de France, 1960.

688   Madison, Gary B. "The ambiguous philosophy of Merleau-Ponty." *Philosophical Studies* (Maynooth), vol. XXII, 1974, pp. 63-77.

689   Martino, Eutimio. "El pessimismo relativo del último Merleau-Ponty. Apuntes de su curso 1958-1959 en el Collège de France." *Pensamiento*, vol. XXVI, no. 101, jan.-March 1970, pp. 73-88.

690   *Mediations*. "Hommage à Maurice Merleau-Ponty." *Mediations*, no. 4, Winter 1961-1962.

GENERAL DISCUSSION

691 Mepham, John. "L'homme connu." *Adam. International Review*, vol. XXXVII, nos. 364-366, 1972, pp. 98-102.

692 *Merleau-Ponty*, Maurice. [special issue] *Aut Aut*, no. 66, Nov. 1961, pp. 481-576.

693 *Merleau-Ponty*, Maurice. [special issue] *Les Temps Modernes*, 17e année, nos. 184-185, octobre-novembre 1961, pp. 193-436.

694 *Merleau-Ponty*. [Special issue.] *L'Arc*, no. 46, 1971.

695 Métraux, Alexandre. "Vorwart," to M. Merleau-Ponty, *Vorlesungen, I: Schrift für die Kandidatur am Collège de France. Lob der Philosophie. Vorlesungszusammenfassungen: Collège de France 1952-1960. Die Humanwissenschaften und die Phänomenologie*. Aus. d. Franz. ubers. u. eingef. durch e. Vorw. von Alexandre Metraux. (Phänomenologisch-psychologische Forschungen, 9). Berlin, New York: de Gruyter, 1973, xxviii-407p.

696 Montefiore, Alan. "Conversations with philosophers--Alan Montefiore looks with Brian Magee at the work done by foreign philosophers." *The Listener*, vol. 85, no. 2188, March 4, 1971, pp. 267-271.

697 Montull, Tomas. "Maurice Merleau-Ponty y su filosofía." *Estudios Filosóficos*, vol. XI, 1962, pp. 371-414; and *Ibid.*, vol. XII, 1963, pp. 81-133.

698 Moreau, Joseph. "Extériorité et transcendance." *Teoresi*, vol. XXVIII, Jan.-June 1973, pp. 3-23.

699 Muglioni, J. "Merleau-Ponty fut-il philosophe?" *Revue Socialiste*, no. 146, octobre 1961, pp. 272-275.

700 Murguia, Adolfo. "Acerca de la muerte de la filosofia." *Revista de Occidente*, vol. XXXIX, no. 116, Nov. 1972, pp. 234-243.

701 Niel, André. *Les Grands appels de l'humanisme contemporain. Christianisme, marxisme, évolutionisme, existentialisme... et après?* Paris: Edition "Courrier du Livre," 1966. 136p.

702 Olafson, Frederick A. "Maurice Merleau-Ponty," pp. 279-282 in *The Encyclopedia of Philosophy*. Ed. Paul Edwards. New York: The Macmillan Co. and The Free Press, vol. 5, 1967.

703   Ollero Tassara, Andrès. "Merleau-Ponty." *Gran Enciclopedia Rialp*. Madrid: Rialp, 1972.

704   Papi, Fulvio. "Introduzione," to *Saggio sulla natura*, by F. J. E. Woodbrige. Trans. by Francisco Tato. Milano: Bompiani, 1956.

705   Pejovic, D. "Maurice Merleau-Ponty." *Praxis* (Zagreb), vol. I, nos. 2-3, 1965, pp. 339-350.

706   Pettit, Philip. "French philosophy." *Cambridge Review*, vol. 94, no. 2214, June 8, 1973, pp. 178-180.

707   *Philosophie et littérature*. Deuxième colloque de la société britannique de philosophie de langue française. Hull: Fretwells, Ltd., 1963. 48p.

708   P.P. "Merleau-Ponty." *Giornale Critico della Filosofia Italiana*, vol. 42, 1963, pp. 426-428.

709   Revel, Jean-François. *Pourquoi des philosophes?* Paris: Jean-Jacques Pauvert, 1964. 184p.

710   Revel, Jean-François. "Appendice 3. Un roi sans couronne," in *Pourquoi des philosophes? 2. La cabale des dévots*. (No. 17: Libertés). Edition augmentée. Paris: Jean-Jacques Pauvert, 1965. 302p.

711   Revel, Jean-François. "Un roi sans couronne: Maurice Merleau-Ponty," pp. 216-220, in *Contre-censures. Politique, religion, culture et masse, art et critique d'art, enseignement, avant-garde, philosophie et sciences humaines, auteurs incompris, antisémitisme*. Paris: Jean-Jacques Pauvert, 1966. 389p.

712   *Revue Internationale de Philosophie*, vol. III, no. 9, 1949, "L'existentialisme devant l'opinion philosophique."

713   Richir, Marc. "La défénestration." *L'Arc*, no. 46, 1971, pp. 31-42.

714   Richir, Marc. "Phénoménalisation, distorsion, logologie. Essai sur la dernière pensée de Merleau-Ponty." *Textures* (Brainc-l'Alleud), vol. IV, no. 4, 1972, pp. 63-114.

715   Ricoeur, Paul. "L'humanité de l'homme: contribution de la philosophie française contemporaine." *Studium Generale*, Heft 5, 1962, pp. 309-323.

716   Russo, F. "Cosmologie du XXe siècle." *Archives de Philosophie*, vol. XXX, juillet-septembre 1967, pp. 398-410.

   Saffirio, Guido. See *Phénoménologie de la Perception*, (No. 401).

717   Said, Edward K. "Labyrinth of incarnation: The essays of Maurice Merleau-Ponty." *Kenyon Review*, vol. XXIX, no. 1, Jan. 1967, pp. 54-68.

718   Sartre, Jean-Paul. "Merleau-Ponty vivant." *Les Temps Modernes*, 17e année, nos. 184-185, octobre-novembre 1961, pp. 304-376. Reprinted in *Situations IV*. Paris: Gallimard, 1964. English trans. by Benita Eisler, *Situations*, pp. 156-226. New York: Braziller, Inc. 1966.

719   Sauvage, Micheline. *L'Aventure philosophique*. Paris: Buchet/Chastel, 1966, xiii-328p.

   Schmitt, Richard. See *Phenomenology of Perception* (No. 402).

720   Schrader, George (ed.). *Existential Philosophers: Kierkegaard to Merleau-Ponty*. See <u>CARR</u> (No. 645).

721   Schrag, Calvin O. *Experience and Being*. Evanston, Ill.: Northwestern University Press, 1969.

722   Scop, Celia. "Paris letter." *Partisan Review*, vol. XIV, no. 3, June 1947, pp. 278-284.

723   Semerari, Giuseppe. "M. Merleau-Ponty," in *Enciclopedia Filosofica* (2a), vol. 4, cols. 550-552. Firenze: Sansoni, 1957.

724   Sheridan, James F. *Once More from the Middle. A Philosophical Anthropology*. Athens, Ohio: Ohio University Press, 1973.

725   Smolko, John F. "Maurice Merleau-Ponty and philosophy," pp. 353-384 in John K. Ryan, ed., *Twentieth Century Thinkers. Studies in the Work of 17 Modern Philosophers*, edited and with an introduction by John K. Ryan. Staten Island, N. Y.: Alba House, a division of St. Paul's Publications, 1965.

726   Spiegelberg, Herbert. "The Phenomenological philosophy of Maurice Merleau-Ponty," pp. 516-560 in vol. 2, *The Phenomenological Movement. A Historical Introduction*. The Hague: Martinus Nijhoff, 1960.

727   Sturani, Enrico. "Letture di Merleau-Ponty."
        Rivista di Filosofia, vol. 58, April-June 1967,
        pp. 164-182.

728   Symposium. "Existentialist thought and contemporary
        philosophy in the West." *Journal of Philosophy*,
        vol. LIII, Nov. 1956, pp. 739-771.

729   *Temps Modernes* (Les). Special number devoted to
        Merleau-Ponty. 17e année, nos. 184-185, octobre-
        novembre 1961, pp. 193-436.

730   Terlin, J. "Maurice Merleau-Ponty." *De Vlaamse
        Gids*, vol. 45, no. 12, Dec. 1969, pp. 801-809.

731   Tijeras, E. "Decimo aniversario de su muerte, Merleau-
        Ponty y la interrogación filosofica." *Informa-
        ciones de las Artes y las Letras*, no. 148, May 6,
        1971, p. 16.

732   Tilliette, Xavier. "Merleau-Pontys Philosophie der
        Endlichkeit." *Dokumente*, vol. XVII, 1961, pp. 271-
        282.

733   Tilliette, Xavier. "Die Philosophie Merleau-Pontys."
        Dokumente, vol. XXII, 1966, pp. 105-110.

734   Tilliette, Xavier. "Merleau-Ponty ou la mesure de
        l'homme." *Archives de Philosophie*, vol. XXIV, nos.
        3-4, juillet-décembre 1961, pp. 399-413.

735   Tilliette, Xavier. "Merleau-Ponty o la medida del
        hombre." *Razon y Fe*, tomo 165, no. 769, Feb. 1962,
        pp. 127-136.

736   Tilliette, Xavier. "Une philosophie sans absolu:
        Maurice Merleau-Ponty, 1908-1961." *Etudes*, tome
        305, septembre 1961, pp. 215-229.

737   Tilliette, Xavier. "Una filosofia viva: Maurice
        Merleau-Ponty (1908-1961)." *Civiltà Cattolica*,
        vol. 123, II, 1972, pp. 554-563.

738   Trotignon, Pierre. *Les Philosophes français
        d'aujourd'hui*. Paris: Presses Universitaires de
        France, 1967.

739   Uscatescu, Jorge. "Espacio, tiempo, imagen."
        Estafeta Literaria, no. 502, Oct. 15, 1972, pp. 4-9.

740   Valentini, Francesco. "Filosofia della corporeita,"
        pp. 43-93 in *La Filosofia francese contemporanea*.
        Milano: Feltrinelli, 1958.

GENERAL DISCUSSION

741   Vinkenoog, Simon. "Onze correspondent meldt: Parijs." *Litterair Paspoort*, no. 90, Oct. 1955, pp. 187-188.

742   Vuillemin, Jules. "La méthode indirecte de Merleau-Ponty." *Critique*, no. 211, décembre 1964, pp. 1007-1016. [Special number devoted to Merleau-Ponty entitled: *Présence de Merleau-Ponty*.]

743   Waelhens, Alphonse de. "Over de betekenis van het oeuvre van Merleau-Ponty." *Tijdschrift voor Filosofie*, vol. XII, 1950, pp. 477-503.

744   Waelhens, Alphonse de. *La Philosophie et les expériences naturelles*. [Dedicated to the memory of Merleau-Ponty.] The Hague: Martinus Nijhoff, 1961.

745   Waelhens, Alphonse de. "Situation de Merleau-Ponty." *Les Temps Modernes*, 17e année, nos. 184-185, octobre-novembre 1961, pp. 377-398. English trans. by Rosemary Lauer, "The Philosophical position of Merleau-Ponty," *Philosophy Today*, vol. VII, no. 2, Summer 1963, pp. 134-149.

746   Waelhens, Alphonse de. "Maurice Merleau-Ponty." *Revista Portuguesa de Filosofia*, vol. XVIII, 1962, pp. 176-186.

747   Waelhens, Alphonse de. "La philosophie de Merleau-Ponty," pp. 329-341, in *Les Philosophes français d'aujourd'hui par eux-mêmes*. Textes recueillis et présentés par G. Deledalle et D. Huisman. Paris: C. D. U., 1963.

748   Wahl, Jean. "Cette pensée. . . ." *Les Temps Modernes*, 17e année, nos. 184-185, octobre-novembre 1961, pp. 399-436. [Special commemorative issue.]

749   Wahl, Jean. "La situation présente de la philosophie française," in *L'Activité philosophique contemporaine en France et aux Etats-Unis*, vol. 2. Paris: Presses Universitaires de France, 1950.

750   Waldenfels, Bernhard. "Gedenken an Maurice Merelau-Ponty." *Zeitschrift für Philosophische Forschung*, vol. XVI, 1962, pp. 406-413.

751   Warnock, Mary. "Laying the foundations." *New Society*, vol. IX, no. 254, Aug. 10, 1967, pp. 198-199.

752   Warnock, Mary. "Maurice Merleau-Ponty," pp. 71-91 in *Existentialism*. London-Oxford-New York: Oxford University Press, 1970.

753   West, Paul. *The Wine of Absurdity. Essays on Literature and Consolation*. University Park and London: The Pennsylvania State University Press, 1966. 249p.

754   Wild, John. "In behalf of the Author (Merleau-Ponty)." *Pacific Philosophy Forum*, vol. III, 1964, pp. 101-104.

755   Winthrop, Henry. "Existential and phenomenological frontiers." *The Journal of Existentialism*, vol. VI, 1966, pp. 459-486.

755a Yolton, John. *Thinking and Perceiving. A Study in the Philosophy of Mind*. La Salle, Ill.: The Open Court Publishing Co., 1961.

SECTION FIVE:

ITEMS ARRANGED BY PROPER NAMES

ALAIN

756 Reboul, Olivier. "Imaginer et percevoir: Alain, la Gestaltthéorie et Merleau-Ponty," pp. 106-114, in *L'Homme et ses passions d'après Alain*. 2 vols. Paris: Presses Universitaires de France, 1968.

AQUINAS

757 Jelly, F. "A Thomist Dialogue with Merleau-Ponty." *Dominicans*, vol. LII, Fall 1967, pp. 242-250.

758 Sweeney, Leo. "Aquinas or philosophers of subjectivity." *The Modern Schoolman*, vol. 47, 1969, pp. 57-70.

ARISTOTLE

759 Mansion, Suzanne. "Aristotle and French phenomenology." *International Philosophical Quarterly*, vol. IV, no. 2, May 1964, pp. 183-199.

ARON, Raymond

760 Aron, Raymond. *L'Opium des intellectuels*. Paris: Gallimard, 1955. English trans. T. Kilmartin, *The Opium of the Intellectuals*. New York: Norton, 1962.

761 LeBlond, Jean-Marie. "Le sens de l'histoire et l'action politique." *Etudes*, tome 287, novembre 1955, pp. 209-219.

762 Nadeau, Maruice. "MM. Aron, Merleau-Ponty et les intellectuels." *Les Lettres Nouvelles*, vol. III, no. 28, juin 1955, pp. 892-903.

763 Patri, Aimé. "De l'opium des intellectuels à la cure de désintoxication." *Preuves*, 53 année, no. 53, juillet 1955, pp. 81-85.

AUSTIN

Fairchild, David Lawrence. See Dissertations (No. 282).

BARTH, Karl

764   Zuidema, S. U. "Een confrontatie tussen Barths theologische theologie en Merleau-Pontys filosofische filosofie." *Philosophia Reformata*, vol. XXIV, pp. 90-96.

BERGSON, Henri

765   Burgers, Antoon. "De houding van Bergson en Merleau-Ponty ten opzichte van de wetenschappen." *Tijdschrift voor Filosofie*, vol. XXVII, June 1965, pp. 262-297.

Fressin, Augustin. See French Books, and Dissertation (Nos. 172 and 283).

766   Scharfstein, Ben-Ami. "Bergson and Merleau-Ponty: A preliminary comparison." *Journal of Philosophy*, vol. LII, no. 4, July 7, 1955, pp. 380-386.

BERKELEY, George

767   Moreau, André. "Merleau-Ponty et Berkeley." *Dialogue*, vol. V, no. 3, Dec. 1966, pp. 418-424.

CAMUS, Albert

768   Weyembergh, Maurice. "Merleau-Ponty et Camus. Humanisme et terreur et *Ni Victimes ni bourreaux*." *Annales de l'Institut de Philosophie*, 1971, pp. 53-99.

CEZANNE, Paul

769   Bate, Michèle. "The phenomenologist as art critic: Merleau-Ponty and Cézanne." *The British Journal of Aesthetics*, vol. 14, no. 4, Autumn 1974, pp. 344-350.

Joseph, Audrey Bendermann. See Dissertation (No. 299)

CLAUDEL, Paul

770   Wahl, Jean. "Maurice Merleau-Ponty et la présence de Claudel." *Bulletin de la Société Paul Claudel*, no. 11, octobre 1962,

DESCARTES, René

Besson, Françoise Gisèle. See Dissertation (No. 262)

Cobb, R. Ellen. See Dissertation (No. 272)

DESCARTES

Jabbour, Victorine. See Dissertation (No. 297).

Morgan, Kathryn Pauly. See Dissertation (No. 316)

ELIOT, T. S.

771 Kumar, Jitendra. "Poesia e percezione: Eliot e Merleau-Ponty." *Il Verri*, no. 31, Dec. 1969, pp. 60-82.

FARBER, Marvin

772 Roth, John K. "Farber's critique of Merleau-Ponty." *The Southern Journal of Philosophy*, vol. VIII, no. 1, Spring 1970, pp. 83-89.

FICHTE

773 Schulte, G. "Vomm Sinn der Wahrnehmung. Die Wissenschaftslehre Fichtes und Merleau-Pontys *Phänomenologie der Wahrnehmung.*" *Tijdschrift voor Filosofie*, vol. XXXI, Dec. 1969, pp. 732-738.

DEWEY, John

Kestenbaum, Victor. "An interpretation of Dewey's notion of habit from the perspective of Merleau-Ponty's phenomenology of the habitual body." See Dissertation (No. 300).

GRODDECK, Georg

774 Lapointe, François H. "The unity of the pre-reflective. Maurice Merleau-Ponty and Georg Groddeck." *Human Inquiries: The Review of Existential Psychology and Psychiatry*, vol. XI, Spring 1971, pp. 169-184.

HABERMAS, Jürgen

775 Walter, Emil H. "Die prekäre Vermittlung von Theorie und Praxis in unserer nachrevolutionären Epoche. Anmerkungen zur Geschichtsphilosophie Maurice Merleau-Pontys and Jürgen Habermas." *Archiv für Rechts- und Sozialphilosophie*, vol. LIII, 1967, pp. 415-430.

HEGEL

776 Cooper, F. B. M. "Hegelian elements in Merleau-Ponty's *Structure of Behavior.*" *International Philosophical Quarterly*, vol. XV, no. 4, Dec. 1975.

HEIDEGGER, Martin

777   Boehm, R. "Chiasme. Merleau-Ponty and Heidegger,"
           pp. 369-393 in *Durchblicke: Martin Heidegger zum
           80. Geburtstag*. Frankfurt am Main: Klostermann,
           1970.

778   Camele, Anthony M. "Time in Merleau-Ponty and
           Heidegger." *Philosophy Today*, vol. XIX, no. 3,
           Fall 1975, pp. 256-268.

           Kaelin, Eugene. See Aesthetics (No. 894).

779   Piorkowski, Henry. See HUSSERL (No. 792).

780   Waelhens, Alphonse de. "Heidegger et Sartre."
           Deucalion, vol. I, 1946.

HUSSERL, Edmund

781   Berger, Gaston. "L'originalité de la phénoménolo-
           gie." *Les Etudes Philosophiques*, vol. IX, 1954,
           pp. 249-259.

782   Brand, G. *Die Lebenswelt. Eine Philosophie des
           konkretes Apriori*. Berlin: Walter de Gruyter,
           1970.

           Bruzina, Ronald C. See Dissertation (No. 267).

           Bruzina, Ronald C. "Merleau-Ponty and Husserl: the
           idea of science," pp. 160-174, in English Books,
           Gillan (No. 135).

           Busch, T. W. See Dissertation (No. 269).

           Cunningham, Suzanne M. See Dissertation (No. 274).

783   Devettere, Raymond J. "Merleau-Ponty and the
           Husserlian reductions." *Philosophy Today*, vol.
           XVII, Winter 1973, pp. 297-308.

           Dreyfus, Hubert L. See Dissertation (No. 278).

784   Fragata, Julio. "Husserl e a filosofia da existen-
           cia." *Revista Portuguesa de Filosofia*, vol. XXI,
           1964, pp. 17-34.

785   Gurwitsch, Aron. "Discussion: The last work of
           Edmund Husserl, (I, II). *Philosophy and Phenome-
           nological Research*, vol. XVII, 1957, pp. 370-378.

786   Holenstein, Elmard. "Passive Genesis: Eine Begriffs-analytische Studie." *Tijdschrift voor Filosofie*, vol. XXXIII, March 1971, pp. 112-153.

787   Holenstein, Elmard. *Phänomenologie der Assoziation. Zu Struktur und Funktion eines Grundprinzips der passiven Genesis bei E. Husserl*. The Hague: Martinus Nijhoff, 1972.

788   Kwant, Remy C. "Merleau-Ponty's criticism of Husserl's eidetic reduction," pp. 393-408 in Joseph J. Kockelmans, ed., *Phenomenology*. Garden City: Doubleday, 1967. [Reprinted from Kwant's *From Phenomenology to Metaphysics*, pp. 156-169.]

789   Marini, A. "Psicologia e fenomenologia in Husserl e Merleau-Ponty." *Aut Aut*, no. 66, Nov. 1961, pp. 539-551.

Murphy, Richard T.   See Dissertation (No. 317).

790   Murphy, Richard T. "A metaphysical critique of method: Husserl and Merleau-Ponty." *Boston College Studies in Philosophy*, vol. 1, 1966, pp. 175-207. Reprinted in *The Quest for the Absolute*, ed. by F. J. Adelmann. The Hague: Martinus Nijhoff, 1966, pp. 175-207.

791   Pietersma, Henry. "Husserl's concept of philosophy." *Dialogue*, vol. V, no. 3, Dec. 1966, pp. 425-442.

792   Piorkowski, Henry. "The path of phenomenology: Husserl, Heidegger, Sartre, Merleau-Ponty." *Duns Scotus Philosophical Association*, vol. XXX, 1966, pp. 177-221.

Rauch, Leo.   See Dissertation (No. 325).

793   Spicker, Stuart. "Inner time and live-through time: Husserl and Merleau-Ponty." *Journal of the British Society for Phenomenology*, vol. IV, no. 3, October 1973, pp. 235-248. See Time.

794   Spiegelberg, Herbert. "Husserl's phenomenology and existentialism." *The Journal of Philosophy*, vol. LII, no. 2, Jan. 21, 1960, pp. 62-74.

Taylor, Darrell.   See Dissertation (No. 334).

795   Thévenaz, Pierre. "Qu'est-ce que la phénoménologie?" *Revue de Théologie et de Philosophie*, 3e série, 1952, pp. 294-316.

796 Thévenaz, Pierre. *De Husserl à Merleau-Ponty. Qu'est-ce que la phénoménologie?* Avec une introduction de Jean Brun. Neuchâtel: Editions de la Baconnière, 1966. 118p. English trans, *What is Phenomenology? and Other Essays,* edited with an introduction [and notes] by James M. Edie. Preface by John Wild. Chicago: Quadrangle Books, 1963. 191p.

797 Van Breda, H. "Maurice Merleau-Ponty et les archives Husserl à Louvain." *Revue de Métaphysique et de Morale,* 67e année, no. 4, octobre-décembre 1962, pp. 410-431.

Vircilio, Domenico. "Le scienze umane la fenomenologia de Husserl a Merleau-Ponty." *Teorisi,* vol. XXV, 1970, pp. 235-273.

JAMES, William

799 Tibbets, Paul. "William James and the doctrine of 'pure experience'." *University of Dayton Review,* vol. VIII, no. 1, Summer 1971, pp. 43-58.

KANT, Immanuel

800 Negri, A. "Lo schematismo kantiano e la fenomenologia esistenzialistica." *La Cultura,* vol. IV, 1966, pp. 468-497.

KOESTLER, Arthur

Desgraupes, P. See Humanisme et Terreur (No. 434).

KOJEVE, Aleandre

801 Sotelo, Ignacio. "El silencio de Alexandre Kojève." *Revista de Occidente,* vol. XX, no. 60, March 1968, pp. 363-371.

LACAN, Jacques

802 Lacan, Jacques. "Maurice Merleau-Ponty." *Les Temps Modernes,* 17e année, nos. 184-185, octobre-novembre 1961, pp. 245-254.

LAVELLE, Louis

Penati, Giancarlo. See Italian Books (No. 229).

LEFORT, Claude

803 Howard, Dick. "Introduction to Lefort." *Telos,* no. 22, Winter 1974-1975, pp. 2-30.

LEVI-STRAUSS, Claude

804   Boon, James A. "Interpretations and conclusions: Through literary correspondences toward a cross-cultural *esprit*," pp. 209-231, in *From Symbolism to Structuralism. Lévi-Strauss in a Literary Tradition.* Oxford: Basil Blackwell, 1972.

805   Mepham, John. "L'homme connu." *Adam. International Review*, vol. XXXVII, nos. 364-366, 1972, pp. 98-102.

806   Lefeuvre, M. "Musique et peinture, ou Lévi-Strauss et Merleau-Ponty." *Etudes*, CCCXL, janvier-juin 1974, pp. 727-735.

807   Lévi-Strauss, Claude. "De quelques rencontres." *L'Arc*, no. 46, 1971, pp. 43-47.

808   Poole, Roger C. "Indirect communications. 2: Merleau-Ponty and Lévi-Strauss." *New Blackfriars*, vol. 47, no. 555, 1966, pp. 594-604.

LEVINAS, Emmanuel

809   De Sanctis, G. B. "L'estetica di due fenomenologi: Lévinas e Merleau-Ponty." *Rivista di Studi Crociani*, vol. IX, 1972, pp. 26-43.

LUKÁCS, Georg

810   Furter, Pierre. "La pensée de Georg Lukács en France." *Revue de Théologie et de Philosophie*, 3e série, tome IX, no. 4, 1961, pp. 353-361.

811   Gurmendez, C. "Dos estéticas, M. Merleau-Ponty y Georg Lukács." *Revista de Occidente*, vol. XXIV, 1965, pp. 363-368.

812   Lukács, Georg. See Garaudy, French Books (No. 175).

813   Paci, Enzo. "Merleau-Ponty, Lukács e il problema della dialettica." *Aut Aut*, no. 66, Nov. 1961, pp. 498-516.

814   Spender, Stephen. "With Lukács in Budapest." *Encounter*, vol. XXIII, no. 6, Dec. 1964, pp. 53-57.

MALRAUX, André

815   Morawski, Stefan. *L'Absolu et la forme. L'esthétique d'André Malraux.* Trans. from the Polish by Yolande Lamy-Grun. Paris: Klincksieck, 1972.

MARCEL, Gabriel

816   Cromp, Germaine. "Le rapport âme-corps chez le premier Marcel." *Dialogue*, vol. VIII, no. 3, Dec. 1969, pp. 445-459.

817   Gillan, Garth. "The question of embodiment: Marcel and Merleau-Ponty." *The Philosophy of Gabriel Marcel*, vol. 15 of The Library of Living Philosophers, Paul A. Schilpp, editor. La Salle, Ill.: The Open Court Pub. Co. 1976.

MARTINET, A.

818   Charron, Ghyslain. "Du langage: la linguistique de Martinet et la phénoménologie de Merleau-Ponty." *Revue de l'Université d'Ottawa*, vol. XXXX, April-June 1970, pp. 260-284.

819   Charron, Ghyslain. "Du langage. Confrontation d'une approche structurale et d'une approche phénoménologique: A. Martinet et M. Merleau-Ponty." *Revue Philosophique de Louvain*, vol. 67, 1969, pp. 676-687.

Charron, Ghyslain. See French Books (No. 168).

MARX, Karl

820   Brockelman, P. T. "Sibling rivalry: The early Marx and some existentialists." *Philosophy Today*, vol. XIII, 1969, pp. 250-262.

MAURRAS, Charles

821   Lysis. "Merleau-Ponty, critique de Charles Maurras." *La Nation Française*, no. 502, 7 juillet 1965, pp. 14-15.

MOREAU, J.

822   Devaux, André. "Idéalisme critique et positivisme phénoménologique: L'esquisse d'un dialogue entre M. Joseph Moreau et Maurice Merleau-Ponty." *Giornale di Metafisica*, vol. XVII, 1962, pp. 79-91.

PIAGET, Jean

823   Piaget, Jean. *Sagesse et illusions de la philosophie*. Paris: Presses Universitaires de France, 1965. English trans. by Wolfe Mays, *Insights and illusions of Philosophy*. New York, Cleveland: The World Publishing Co., 1971.

824   Zaner, Richard M. "Piaget and Merleau-Ponty: A study in convergence." *Review of Existential Psychology and Psychiatry*, vol. VI, no. 1, Winter 1966, pp. 7-23.

PLATO

Dallery, Robert Carleton. See Dissertation (No. 275).

POLANYI, M.

825   Grene, Marjorie. "Polanyi et la philosophie française." *Archives de Philosophie*, vol. XXXV, janvier-mars 1972, pp. 3-5.

RYLE, Gilbert

826   Dubois, Pierre. "Ryle et Merleau-Ponty: faut-il exorciser le fantôme qui se cache dans la machine humaine?" *Revue Philosophique de la France et de l'Etranger*, vol. 95, juillet-septembre 1970, pp. 299-317.

827   Jacques, J. H. "Exorcising the ghost in the machine." *The Listener*, vol. 74, no. 1893, July 8, 1965, pp. 49-51.

828   Martinelli, Lucien. "Etude critique des *Cahiers de Royaumont IV: La philosophie analytique* (Paris, 1963)." *Dialogue*, vol. II, no. 2, Sept. 1963, pp. 206-221.

SARTRE, Jean-Paul

829   Arntz, J. "L'athéisme au nom de l'homme? L'athéisme de J.-P. Sartre et de M. Merleau-Ponty." *Concilium*, no. 16, 1966, pp. 59-64.

830   Arntz, J. "Ateismo en nombre del hombre? J.-P. Sartre y M. Merleau-Ponty." *Concilium*, [Spanish edition], no. 16, 1966, pp. 224-230.

831   Aron, Raymond. *L'Opium des intellectuels*. Paris: Gallimard, 1955.

832   Aron, Raymond. "Of passions and polemics." *Encounter*, vol. XXXIV, no. 5, May 1970, pp. 49-55.

833   Bannon, John F. "Merleau-Ponty and Sartre," pp. 229-243 in Books (No. 127).

833a   Beauvoir, Simone de. See *Les Aventures* (No. 473).

834   Biemel, Walter. "Sartres Widerpart: Maurice Merleau-Ponty in Deutschland." *Die Zeit*, vol. XXI, no. 42, 1966, p. 29.

835   Bonomi, Andrea. "La polemica contra Sartre." *Aut Aut*, no. 66, 1961, pp. 562-567.

836   Burnier, Michel-Antoine. *Les existentialistes et la politique*. Paris: Gallimard, 1966. 189p. English trans. by Bernard Murchland, *Choice of Action. The French Existentialists on the Political Front Line*. Additional chapter by Bernard Murchland, "Sartre and Camus: The Anatomy of a quarrel." New York: Random House, 1968.

837   Capizzi, Antonio. "Su una divergenza fra Sartre e Merleau-Ponty." *La Cultura*, vol. VI, 1968, pp. 147-150.

838   Carlini, Armando. "Una difésa di Sartre." *Idea*, vol. VI, no. 23, June 6, 1954, p. 1.

839   Daniels, Graham. "Sartre and Merleau-Ponty: An existentialist quarrel." *French Studies*, vol. XXIV, 1970, pp. 379-392.

840   Dillon, Martin C. "Sartre on the phenomenal body and Merleau-Ponty's critique." *Journal of the British Society for Phenomenology*, vol. V, no. 2, May 1974, pp. 144-157.

841   Dreyfus, Nina. "A propos de 'Merleau-Ponty vivant'." *Mercure de France*, no. 1184, avril 1962, pp. 928-936.

842   Dufrenne, Mikel. "Les aventures de la dialectique ou les avatars d'une amitié philosophique." *Combat*, 29 septembre 1955. Reprinted in *Jalons*, pp. 169-173. The Hague: Martinus Nijhoff, 1966. See Les Aventures.

Dunne, R. "The validity of Merleau-Ponty's criticism of Sartre's Marxism." See Dissertation (No. 279).

Flynn, Bernard. "The question of ontology: Sartre and Merleau-Ponty," pp. 114-126. See Gillan English Books (No. 135).

Gahamanyi, Célestin. "La conception de la liberté chez Sartre et Merleau-Ponty." See Dissertation (No. 286).

SARTRE

Gallagher, Donald K. "Ontology and eidos: A critical study of Sartre and Merleau-Ponty." See Dissertation (No. 287).

843 Grene, Marjorie. "The aesthetic dialogue of Sartre and Merleau-Ponty." *Journal of the British Society for Phenomenology*, vol. I, May 1970, pp. 59-70.

844 Holz, Hans Heinz. "Nachwort zur deutschen Übersetzung von 'Merleau-Ponty vivant'." Wiesbaden, 1962.

845 Hyppolite, Jean. "Merleau-Ponty vivant." *Les Temps Modernes*, 17e année, nos. 184-185, octobre-novembre 1961, pp. 228-244.

Kwant, Remy C. "Merleau-Ponty and Sartre," pp. 203-223 in Books English (No. 139).

846 Lefort, Claude. "De la réponse à la question." *Les Temps Modernes*, 9e année, no. 101, février 1954, pp. 157-184.

847 Lessing, Arthur. "Sartre and Merleau-Ponty." *Barat Review*, vol. V, 1970, pp. 55-59.

848 Lessing, Arthur. "Walking in the world: Sartre and Merleau-Ponty." *Human Inquiries*, vol. XI, nos. 1-2, Summer-Fall 1971, pp. 43-56.

849 Maier, Willi. *Das Problem der Leiblickheit bei Sartre und Merleau-Ponty.* See German Books (No. 206).

850 Moravia, S. "La crisi della generazione sartriana." *Rivista di Filosofia*, vol. LVIII, Oct.-Dec. 1967, pp. 426-470.

851 Moreland, John M. "For-itself and in-itself in Sartre and Merleau-Ponty." *Philosophy Today*, vol. XVII, Winter 1973, pp. 311-318.

Murphy, Richard T. "Phenomenology and the dialectic: A study of prereflexive consciousness in the phenomenological theories of Husserl, Sartre and Merleau-Ponty." See Dissertation (No. 317).

Nadeau, Maurice. See ARON (No. 762).

852 O'Neill, John. "Situation and temporality." *Philosophy and Phenomenological Research*, vol. XXVIII, March 1968, pp. 413-422.

853   Palmier, Jean-Michel. "Le dialogue avec Sartre ou l'histoire d'une amitié." *Le Monde* [*des Livres*], no. 7857, 18 avril 1970, pp. 4-5.

854   Parain, Brice. "Querelle de khagneux." *Monde Nouveau-Paru*, vol. XI, no. 92, Sept. 1955, pp. 45-51.

855   Patocka, J. "Die Kritik des psychologischen Objektivismus und das Problem der phänomenologischen Psychologie bei Sartre und Merleau-Ponty," pp. 175-184, in *Akten 14th International Congress of Philosophy*, Vienna, Sept. 2-9, 1968. *Proceedings of the 14th International Congress of Philosophy*. Vienna: Herder, 1968. xv-688p.

856   Patri, Aimé. "Journal des idées: Sartre et Merleau-Ponty." *Preuves*, no. 135, mai 1962, pp. 84-86.

857   Pingaud, Bernard. "Merleau-Ponty, Sartre et la littérature." *L'Arc*, no. 46, 1971, pp. 80-87.

Piorkowski, Henry. "The path of phenomenology." See HUSSERL (No. 792).

858   Podleck, A. *Der Leib als Weise des in-der-Welt-Seins*. Bonn: Bouvier, 1956.

Quilliot, R. "De Nekrassov à Merleau-Ponty." See LES AVENTURES DE (No. 498).

Rabil, Albert. "Merleau-Ponty and Sartrian existentialism," pp. 116-140 in Books (No. 156).

859   Rauch, Leo. "Sartre, Merleau-Ponty and the 'hole in being'." *Philosophical Studies* (Maynooth), vol. XVIII, 1969, pp. 119-132.

860   Sartre, Jean-Paul. "Merleau-Ponty vivant." *Les Temps Modernes*, 17e année, nos. 184-185, octobre-novembre 1961, pp. 304-376. Reprinted in *Situations IV*. Paris: Gallimard, 1964. English trans. by Benita Eisler, *Situations*, pp. 156-226. New York: Braziller, Inc., 1966.

Senofonte, Ciro. *Sartre e Merleau-Ponty*. See Italian Books (No. 231).

Sheridan, James F. "On ontology and politics: A polemic," see Les Aventures (No. 501).

SARTRE

861 Smith, Colin. "Sartre and Merleau-Ponty: The case for a modified essentialism." *Journal of the British Society for Phenomenology*, vol. I, May 1970, pp. 73-79.

862 Sorel, Jean-Jacques." Merleau-Ponty contre Sartre." *France Observateur*, vol. VI, no. 263, 26 mai 1955, pp. 16-18.

863 Truc, Gonzague. "J.-P. Sartre, M. Merleau-Ponty et l'athéisme radical." *Ecrits de Paris*, no. 131, octobre 1955, pp. 27-31.

864 Waelhens, Alphonse de. "Merleau-Ponty en Sartre." *Tijdschrift voor Filosofie*, vol. XII, 1950, pp. 447-503.

865 Weightman, J. G. "The French debate." *The New Statesman and Nation*, vol. LIII, no. 1329, Sept. 1, 1956, pp. 245-246.

SAUSSURE, Ferdinand de

866 Lagueux, Maurice. "Merleau-Ponty et la linguistique de Saussure." *Dialogue*, vol. IV, no. 3, Dec. 1965, pp. 351-364.

867 Nethold, Ana Maria, ed. *Ferdinand de Saussure*, por e. Beneviste, R. Godel, A. J. Greimas, Hjemslev, J. Starobinsky, R. E. Wells. Ed. selec. y trad. a cargo de A. M. Nethold. Buenos Aires: Siglo Veintiuno Argentina Edit. 1971.

868 Vangroenweghe, Daniel. "Maurice Merleau-Ponty en Ferdinand de Saussure." *Tijdschrift voor Filosofie*, vol. XXXV, Spring 1973, pp. 455-467.

SCHILDER, Paul   See BODY (No. 947)

SKINNER, B. F.

869 Corriveau, Michael. "Phenomenology, psychology, and radical behaviorism: Skinner and Merleau-Ponty." *Journal of Phenomenological Psychology*, vol. III, no. 1, Fall 1972, pp. 7-34.

870 Kvale, Steinar, & Grenness, Carl E. "Skinner and Sartre: Toward a radical phenomenology of behavior?" *Review of Existential Psychology and Psychiatry*, vol. VII, Spring 1967, pp. 128-150.

871 Meyer, Miles W. "Toward a phenomenological theory of learning: The contributions of B. F. Skinner." *Journal of Phenomenological Psychology*, vol. 5, no. 2, Spring 1975, pp. 335-369.

SPINOZA, B.

872 Lessing, Alba. "Spinoza and Merleau-Ponty on human existence." *Proceedings New Mexico-West Texas Philosophical Association*, April 1972, pp. 20-24.

THOMAS (see AQUINAS)

TROTSKY, Leon

873 Lefort, Claude. "La contradiction de Trotsky et le problème révolutionnaire." *Les Temps Modernes*, 4e année, no. 39, 1949, pp. 23-36.

VICO, Giambattista

874 Edie, James M. "Vico and existential philosophy," pp. 483-495 in Giorgio Tagliacozzo, (ed.), *Giambattista Vico. An International Symposium*. Baltimore: The Johns Hopkins Press, 1969.

VIAN, Boris

875 "Un inédit de Boris Vian: Petite géographie humaine de Saint-Germain-des Prés--Quelques autochtones authentiques." *Arts & Loirirs*, no. 24, 9-15 mars, 1966, pp. 66-68.

VOLOSINOV,

876 Carruba, Gerald J. "Some phenomenological aspects of a Marxist philosophy of language." *Kinesis*, vol. VI, no. 2, Spring 1974, pp. 95-112.

Carruba, Gerald J. See Dissertations (No. 271).

WEBER, Max

877 Lukács, Georg. "Max Weber et la sociologie allemande." *La Nouvelle Critique*, 7e année, no. 67, 1955, pp. 77-91.

WHITEHEAD, Alfred N.

878 Hamrick, William S. "Whitehead and Merleau-Ponty: Some moral implications." *Process Studies*, vol. IV, Winter 1974, pp. 235-251.

WHITEHEAD

879 Hamrick, William S. "Body, space, and time in the philosophies of Whitehead and Merleau-Ponty." See Dissertation

880 Mays, Wolfe. "Whitehead and the philosophy of time." *Studium Generale*, vol. XXIII, 1970, pp. 509-524.

WITTGENSTEIN, Ludwig

881 Epstein, Michele F. "The common ground of Merleau-Ponty's and Wittgenstein's philosophy of man." *Journal of the History of Philosophy*, Vol. XIII, no. 2, April 1975, pp. 221-234.

882 Kwant, Remy C. "Merleau-Ponty en Wittgenstein." *Tijdschrift voor Filosofie*, vol. XXXII, March 1970, pp. 3-29.

883 Marsh, James L. "The triumph of ambiguity: Merleau-Ponty and Wittgenstein." *Philosophy Today*, vol. XIX, no. 3, Fall 1975, pp. 243-255.

SECTION SIX

ITEMS ARRANGED BY SUBJECTS

ABSOLUTE (see also GOD)

884   Falco, Fausta. "La fluidificazione dell'assoluto in M. Merleau-Ponty," pp. 405-458 in *Atti dell'Academia delle Scienze di Torino*, Classe di Sc. Mor., Stor., e Filos., vol. 95, 1960-1961, pp. 405-458.

885   Jolivet, Régis. "Le problème de l'absolu dans la philosophie de M. Merleau-Ponty." *Tijdschrift voor Filosofie*, vol. XIX, no. 1, March-June 1957, pp. 530100. Abridge English trans. by M. Delphine and Alphonse Spilly, "The problem of God in the philosophy of Merleau-Ponty," *Philosophy Today*, vol. VII, no. 2, Summer 1963, pp. 150-164.

886   Kwant, Remy C. "De historie en het absolute. Kritische analyse van de opvatting van Merleau-Ponty." See HISTORY (No. 1098).

Sanabria, José Ruben. See GOD (No. 1090).

887   Tilliette, Xavier. "Une philosophie sans absolu: Maurice Merleau-Ponty." *Etudes*, tome 305, septembre 1961, pp. 215-229.

ACT

Fontan, Pierre. "Le primat de l'acte sur l'énoncé." See *Phen. P.* (No. 381).

ACTION

Aubenque, Pierre. "Dialectique et action." See LES AVENTURES (No. 470).

ACTUALITY

888   Burnier, Michel-Antoine. "Actualité de Merleau-Ponty." *Le Magazine Littéraire*, no. 35, décembre 1969, pp. 35-37.

AESTHETICS (and art)

889   Barilli, R. "Merleau-Ponty e l'iperdialettica," pp. 204-239, and "Linguaggio e estetica in Merleau-Ponty," pp. 240-270 in *Per un'estetica mondana*. Bologna: Il Mulino, 1964.

AESTHETICS

Bate, Michèle. "The phenomenologist as art critic:" see CEZANNE (No. 769).

Battaglini, A. "*Senso e non-senso* di Merleau-Ponty e l'estetica fenomenologica italiana." See *Sens et Non-sens* (No. 455).

890 Berger, John. "Arts in society: The sight of a man." *New Society*, vol. XV, no. 394, April 16, 1970, pp. 646-647.

De Sanctis, G. B. "L'estetica di due fenomenologi: Levinas e Merleau-Ponty." See LEVINAS (No. 809).

891 Ecker, David M. "How to think in other categories: The problem of alternative conceptions of aesthetic education." *Journal of Aesthetic Education*, vol. IV, April 1970, pp. 21-36.

892 Fanizza, Franco. "Motivi estetici nella fenomenologia di Merleau-Ponty." *Aut Aut*, no. 66, Nov. 1961, pp. 516-539.

893 Fukada, Susumu. "L'art et le sens. Essai sur vues sur les arts de Merleau-Ponty" (sic) *Bigaku*, vol. XXII, Dec. 1971, pp. 20-33.

Grene, Marjorie. "The aesthetic dialogue of Sartre and Merleau-Ponty." See SARTRE (No. 843).

Gurmendez, C. "Dos estéticas, M. Merleau-Ponty y Georg Lukács." See LUKACS (No. 811).

Joseph, Andrey Bendermann. "Artistic vision and the metaphysical imagination: Toward a phenomenology of aesthetic consciousness." See Dissertation (No. 299).

Kaelin, Eugene. *An Existentialist Aesthetics*. See English Books (No. 138).

894 Kaelin, Eugene. "Notes toward an understanding of Heidegger's aesthetics," pp. 59-92 in Edward N. Lee and Maurice Maldelbaum, (eds.), *Phenomenology and existentialism*. Baltimore: The Johns Hopkins Press, 1967.

895 Kaelin, Eugene. "The visibility of things seen: A phenomenological view of painting." pp. 30-58 in James M. Edie (ed.), *Phenomenological Studies in the Philosophy of Experience*. Chicago: Quadrangle Books, 1965.

896   Kaelin, Eugene. *Art and existence: A Phenomenological Aesthetics*. Lewisburg, Pa.: Bucknell University Press, 1971, c. 1970.

897   Kogan, Jacabo. "Personalidad estetica y actividad creadora." *La Torre*, vol. XII, no. 47, July-Sept. 1964, pp. 65-93.

Kumar, Jitendra. See ELIOT (No. 771).

Kwant, Remy C. *De Stemmen der Stilte. Merleau-Ponty's analyse van de Schilderkunst*. See Dutch Books (No. 253).

898   Kwant, Remy C. *The Phenomenology of Expression*. Pittsburgh: Duquesne University Press, 1970.

899   Lapointe, François. "Selected bibliography on art and aesthetics in Merleau-Ponty." *Philosophy Today*, vol. XVII, no. 4, Winter 1973, pp. 292-296.

Lefeuvre, M. "Musique et peinture, ou Lévi-Strauss et Merleau-Ponty." See LEVI-STRAUSS (No. 806).

900   Levine, Stephen K. "Merleau-Ponty's philosophy of Art." *Man and World*, vol. II, no. 3, Aug. 1969, pp. 438-452.

901   Major, Jean-Louis. "Pensée concrète, art abstrait." *Dialogue*, vol. I, no. 2, 1962, pp. 188-201.

Morawski, Stefan. *L'Absolu et la forme. L'esthétique d'André Malraux*. See MALRAUX (No. 915).

902   Oxenhandler, Neal. "Toward the new aesthetic." *Contemporary Literature*, vol. XI, no. 2, Spring 1970, pp. 169-191.

Place, James G. "Merleau-Ponty's philosophy of painting." See Dissertation (No. 321).

Place, James G. "Merleau-Ponty's and the spirit of painting." See PAINTING (No. 1249).

Schwartzmann, Felix. *Teoria de la expresión*. See EXPRESSION (No. 1075a).

903   Sherman, Susan. "The language of art." *Ikon*, vol. I, no. 3, July 4, 1967, pp. 42-45.

106   AESTHETICS

904   Tilliette, Xavier. "L'esthétique de Merleau-Ponty."
        Rivista di Estetica, vol. XIV, no. 1, Jan.-April
        1969, pp. 102-119.

905   Van Haecht, Louis. "Beauté visible et métaphysique."
        Revue Philosophique de Louvain, février 1962, pp.
        100-117.

906   Viano, Carlo A. "Filosofia, linguaggio e arte in
        Maurice Merleau-Ponty." *Questioni*, no. 1, Jan.-
        Feb. 1955, pp. 25-30.

907   Waelhens, Alphonse de. "Merleau-Ponty philosophe de
        la peinture." *Revue de Métaphysique et de Morale*,
        67e année, no. 4, octobre-décembre 1962, pp. 431-
        449.

        ALIENATION

        Fabian, Rainer. See Dissertation (No. 281).

        AMBIGUITY

        Caillois, Roland. See ELOGE (No. 581).

908   Campbell, Robert. "De l'ambiguité à l'héroisme chez
        Merleau-Ponty." *Cahiers du Sud*, nos. 390-391,
        Octobre-décembre 1966, pp. 273-284.

909   Carlini, Armando. "Filosofia dell'ambiguità e
        ambiguità della filosofia." *Giornale di Meta-
        fisica*, vol. V, 1957, pp. 541-554.

910   Chaix-Ruy, J. "Une philosophie de l'ambiguité, M.
        Merleau-Ponty," in *Les Grands courants de la
        pensée mondiale contemporaine*, T. I. M. F. Sciacca,
        ed. Milano: C. Marzorati, 1958.

911   Derossi, G. "Maurice Merleau-Ponty: dall' 'ambi-
        guità' al transcendentalismo corporeo." *Filo-
        sofia* (Torino), vol. XIV, 1963, pp. 387-411.

912   Dwiggins, C. W. "The phenomenon of ambiguity."
        Man and World, vol. IV, 1971, pp. 270-283.

913   Fergnani, Franco. "Marxismo e 'filosofia dell'ambi-
        guità'," *Il Pensiero Critico*, no. 4, Oct.-Dec.
        1960, pp. 16-65.

        Lacroix, Jean. See General Presentation (No. 676).

914 Lefebvre, Henri. "M. Merleau-Ponty et la philosophie de l'ambiguité." *La Pensée*, no. 68, juillet-août 1956, pp. 44-56; and *Ibid.*, no. 73, mai-juin 1957, pp. 37-52.

Lefebvre, Henri. "Une philosophie de l'ambiguité," pp. 99-106 in Garaudy, Books (No. 175).

Marsh, James L. "The triumph of ambiguity." See WITTGENSTEIN (No. 883).

McCleary, Richard Calverton. See Dissertation (No. 312).

915 Madison, Gary B. "The ambiguous philosophy of Merleau-Ponty." *Philosophical Studies* (Maynooth), vol. XXII, 1974, pp. 63-77.

916 Paci, Enzo. "Ambiguetà e verità in M. Merleau-Ponty," in *Funzione delle scienze e significato dell'uomo*. (Part 3, chapter 3). Milano: Il Saggiatore, 1963. English trans. with an introduction by Paul Piccone and James E. Hansen, *The Function of the Sciences and the Meaning of Man*. Evanston, Ill.: Northwestern University Press, 1972.

917 Rozitchner, Leon. "Merleau-Ponty: la ambigüedad como revelación de la crisis." *Imago Mundi*, vol. III, nos. 11-12, March-June 1956, pp. 199-207.

Silverman, Hugh Jerald. "Existential ambiguity: phenomenology of human nature." See Dissertation (No. 330).

ANALYSIS

Caillois, Roland. See *Deucalion*, Vol. I, 1946, pp. 125-139. See *Phen de la P* (No. 369).

918 Tillman, F. "Phenonenology and philosophical analysis." *International Philosophical Quarterly*, vol. VI, 1966, pp. 465-482.

ANTHROPOLOGY

919 Ram Adhar Mall. "Existentialism as philosophical anthropology." *Philosophical Quarterly* (India), vol. 39, 1966, pp. 199-206.

920 Strasser, Stephen. "De betekenis van Merleau-Ponty voor de wijsgerige anthropologie." *Gawein*, vol. XII, 1964, pp. 208-224. Reprinted in *Bouwstenen voor een filosofische anthropologie*, pp. 313-332. Hilversum/Antwerpen: Paul Brand, 1965.

ANTI-CARTESIANISM

Minhinnick, J. See Dissertation (No. 314).

ANTI COMMUNIST VOGUE

Châtelet, François. "Merleau-Ponty et la dernière mode de l'anticommunisme." See *Les Aventures* (No. 475).

A PRIORI (notion of)

921 Dufrenne, Mikel. *La Notion d'a priori*. Paris: Presses Universitaires de France, 1959. (English trans.)

922 Dufrenne, Mikel. "A priori et philosophie de la nature." *Filosofia* (Torino), vol. XVIII, 1967, pp. 1-14.

ATHEISM (see also: God, Religion, Absolute)

Arntz, J. "Ateismo en nombre del Hombre?" See SARTRE (No. 829).

Arntz, J. "L'athéisme au nom de l'homme?" See SARTRE (No. 830).

923 Capizzi, Antonio. "Figure dell'ateismo francese del dopoguerra [Andre Gide, Jean-Paul Sartre, Albert Camus, Maurice Merleau-Ponty]. *Giornale Critico della Filosofia Italiana*, vol. 45, Oct.-Dec. 1966, pp. 541-586.

924 Daniélou, Jean. *Dialogue avec les existentialistes*, pp. 105-112. Paris: Le Portulan, 1948.

925 Earle, William. "Man as the impossibility of God," pp. 82-112 in *Christianity and Existentialism*. Evanston, Ill.: Northwestern University Press, 1963.

926 Fabro, Cornelio. "Patent atheism in French existentialism," pp. 938-957 in *God in Exile. Modern Atheism. A Study of the Internal Dynamic of Modern Atheism From Its Roots in the Cartesian Cogito to the Present Day*. Trans. from the Italian and edited by A. Gibson. Westminster, Md.: Newman Press, 1968.

Falco, Fausta. See ABSOLUTE (No. 884).

927 Gavaert, J. "Attorno al paradigma della creazione." *Salesiamum*, vol. XXIX, 1967, pp. 701-713.

928   Gerber, Rudolph J. "Causality and atheism." *Proceedings of the Catholic Philosophical Association*, vol. XLIV, 1970, pp. 232-240.

929   Gerber, Rudolph J. "Causality and atheism: The difficulty with the creative God in existential phenomenology." *The Personalist*, vol. LI, Fall 1970, pp. 522-534.

930   Lacroix, Jean. "Sens et valeur de l'athéisme actuel." *Esprit*, 22e année, 1954, pp. 167-191.

       LeBlond, Jean-Marie. See ELOGE (No. 590).

931   Lotz, J. "Ateismo e esistenzialismo, II: L'ateismo in Merleau-Ponty," pp. 321-329 in *L'Ateismo contemporaneo, II*. Torino: Societa Editrice Internazionale, 1968.

932   Lucas Hernández, J. S. "Dimension del hombre en el ateismo contemporáneo." *Revista de Filosofia* (Madrid), vol. XXIII, 1964, pp. 5-49.

933   Luipjen, W. *Phenomenology and Atheism*. Pittsburgh: Duquesne University Press, 1964.

934   Masterson, Patrick. "Existentialism and the rejection of idols," pp. 128-153 in *Atheism and Alienation. A Study of the Philosophical Sources of Contemporary Atheism*. London: Gill and Macmillan, 1971; University of Notre Dame Press, 1972.

935   Montull, Tomas. "El ateismo de Merleau-Ponty." *La Ciencia Tomista*, vol. 90, 1963, pp. 115-181.

       Sanabria, José Ruben. *Filosofia del absoluto. Affirmación y rechazo de Dios en*. . . See GOD (No. 1090).

       Truc, Gonzague. "J.-P. Sartre, M. Merleau-Ponty et l'athéisme radical." See SARTRE (No. 863).

936   Wicker, Brian. "Atheism and the avant-garde." *New Blackfriars*, vol. LI, no. 606, Nov. 1970, pp. 527-535.

       Zeiler, M. Judith. "From contingency to hope." See Dissertation (No. 339).

       BEHAVIOR (see also *La Structure du comportement*)

937   Cazabon, Gilles. "Deux approches antithétiques du problème du comportement." *Revue Philosophique de Louvain*, 67 année, Nov. 1969, pp. 546-581.

110   BEHAVIOR

Corriveau, Michael. See SKINNER (No. 869).

938   Montpellier, Gérard de. "La psychologie est-elle la science du comportement?" *Revue Philosophique de Louvain*, 68e année, mai 1970, pp. 174-192.

O'Connor, Tony. See INTENTIONALITY (No. 1038a).

939   Romanyshyn, Robert D. "Metaphors and human behavior." *Journal of Phenomenological Psychology*, vol. V, no. 2, Spring 1975, pp. 441-460.

Szaszkiewicz, Jerzy. *Relation entre le comportement et la connaissance selon Merleau-Ponty*. See French Books (No. 192).

BEING (see Ontology)

939a   Gillan, Garth. "Interrogative thought. Merleau-Ponty and the degree zero of being." *Sub-stance* 8, Winter 1974, pp. 65-76.

940   Henry, Michel. *L'Essence de la manifestation*. Paris Presses Universitaires de France, 2 vols. 1963. English trans. by G. Etzkorn, *The Essence of Manifestation*. The Hague: Martinus Nijhoff, 1973. 740p.

941   Kwant, Remy C. "The Human body as the self-awareness of being." See BODY (No. 946).

942   Lingus, Alphonso. "Being in the interrogative mood," pp. 78-91 in GILLAN Books, No. 135.

943   Zanni, L. "Fenomenologia dell'essere in Maurice Merleau-Ponty." *Rivista di Filosofia Neo-Scolastica*, vol. 49, nos. 5-6, Sept.-Dec. 1957, pp. 542-549.

Rauch, Leo. See SARTRE (No. 859).

BODY (See also Bodiliness, Embodiment)

Bannan, John F. "The body and perception," pp. 59-86 in *The Philosophy of Merleau-Ponty*. See Books (No. 127).

Barral, Mary Rose. "Merleau-Ponty: The role of the body in interpersonal relations." See Dissertation (No. 260).

Barral, Mary Rose. *The Role of the Body-Subject in Interpersonal Relations*. See Books (No. 130).

942   Barral, Mary Rose. "Merleau-Ponty on the body." *The Southern Journal of Philosophy*, vol. VII, no. 2, Summer 1969, pp. 171-179.

943   Bruaire, Claude. "La dualité du corps et le désespoir de la conscience," pp. 124-140 in *Philosophie du corps*. Paris: Editions du Seuil, 1968.

Cobb, R. Ellen. "The Cartesian principle of self-evidence and Merleau-Ponty's thesis that 'I am my body'." See Dissertation (No. 272).

944   Derossi, Giorgio. "Maurice Merleau-Ponty: dall''ambiguità' al transcendentalismo corporeo." *Filosofia* (Torino), vol. XIV, 1963, pp. 387-411.

Dillon, Martin C. "Sartre on the phenomenal body and Merleau-Ponty's critique." See SARTRE (No. 840).

945   Doubrovsky, Serge. "L'enracinement de la parole dans le corps." *Le Monde [des Livres]*, no. 7857, 18 avril 1970, p. 5.

Eisenberg, Allan Mark. "The function of the intentional body in Merleau-Ponty's *Phenomenology of Perception*." See Dissertation (No. 280).

Gillan, Garth J. "The question of embodiment: Marcel and Merleau-Ponty." See MARCEL (No. 817).

Good, Paul. "Du corps à la chair." See Dissertation (No. 290).

Hamrick, William S. "Body, space, and time in the philosophies of Whitehead and Merleau-Ponty." See WHITEHEAD (No. 879).

Kestenbaum, Victor. "An interpretation of Dewey's notion of habit from the perspective of Merleau-Ponty's phenomenology of the habitual body." See Dissertation (No. 300).

Kwant, Remy C. "Merleau-Ponty's fundamental discovery: The body-subject," pp. 11-30; "Merleau-Ponty's approach to the body-subject," pp. 31-45; "Body and language," pp. 46-62, in *The Phenomenological Philosophy of Merleau-Ponty*. See English Books (No. 139).

946   Kwant, Remy C. "The human body as the self-awareness of being." *Humanitas*, (Pittsburgh), vol. II, Spring 1966, pp. 43-62. Reprinted in *Review of Existential Psychology and Psychiatry*, vol. VIII, no. 2, Spring 1968, pp. 117-134.

BODY

947   Lacas, Pierre-Paul. "Représentation et expression de CORPS; la pensée contemporaine de Schilder à Merleau-Ponty: le secret du corps est-il les profondeurs de l'âme?" *AS (L'Art Sacré)*, no. 1, ler trimestre, 1969, pp. 3-22.

948   Lapointe, François H. "The phenomenal body in the later writings of Merleau-Ponty." *Journal of General Psychology*, vol. 84, April 1971, pp. 251-265.

      Lapointe, François H. "The significance of time in Merleau-Ponty's phenomenology of the body and the world." See TIME (No. 1372).

949   Lapointe, François H. "The objective and the phenomenal body." *Diafora', Rivista Trimestriale Internazionale di Filosofia*, anno 6, nos. 2-3, 1975.

950   Lapointe, François H. "Merleau-Ponty on the body as flesh." *Diafora'. Rivista trimestrale Internazionale di Filosofia e varia Scienza*, anno 4, fasc. 2-3, Spring-Fall 1973, pp. 19-22.

951   Lapointe, François H. "The evolution of Merleau-Ponty's concept of the body." *Journal of Phenomenological Psychology*, vol. V, no. 2, Spring 1975, pp. 389-405.

952   Lefort, Claude. "Le corps, la chair." *L'Arc*, no. 46 1971, pp. 5-18.

953   Maier, W. See Books (No. 206).

954   Maione, Pasquale. "La dimensione archeologica dell'uomo." *Rassegna Scienze Filosofiche*, vol. I, no. 22, 1969, pp. 255-266.

955   Mainetti, José Alberto. *Realidad, fenomeno y misterio del cuerpo*. La Plata: Quiron, 1972.

956   Mbwaki, A. M. "Les notions de structure, de sens et de corps chez M. Merleau-Ponty." *Annuaire de l'Université de Paris*, vol. XXXVIII, 1968, pp. 506-507.

      Meddens, Hans. *Une Phénoménologie du corps*. See Books (No. 187).

957   Montull, Tomas. "Merleau-Ponty: ambigüedad existencial del cuerpo." *Estudios Filosóficos*, vol. XIII, 1964, pp. 271-317.

BODY   113

958   Plügge, Hans. *Das Mensch und sein Leib.* Tübingen: Niemeyer, 1967.

959   Sciacca, Michele Federico. "Il corporeismo di Merleau-Ponty," in *La Filosofia oggi.* Milano: Marzorati, 1947.

       Springer, W. C. "The world and the word in Merleau-Ponty. Toward an existential epistemology and an ontology of the human body." See Dissertation (No. 331).

       Tilliette, Xavier. Le corps et le temps dans la *Phénoménologie de la perception.* See Books, and *Phénoménologie de la Perception* (No. 194).

960   Valentini, Francesco. "Filosofia della corporeità," pp. 43-93 in *La Filosofia francese contemporanea.* Milano: Feltrinelli, 1958.

960a   Waelhens, Alphonse de. "La phénoménologie du corps." *Revue Philosophique de Louvain,* vol. 48, Août 1950, pp. 371-390. English trans. in Nathaniel Lawrence & Daniel O'Connor (eds.), *Readings in Existential Phenomenology,* pp. 149-167.

       Podlech, Adalbert. See German Books (No. 209).

961   Van Peursen, C. A. "Bodiliness: Gehlen, Plessner, Sartre, Merleau-Ponty," ch. 10 in *Body, Soul, Spirit: A Survey of the Body-Mind Problem.* London: Oxford University Press, 1966. English edition translated from the Dutch by Hubert H. Hoskins, with additional matter by the author.

962   Waelhens, Alphonse de. "Le corps: chose ou accès aux choses," pp. 59-70 in *La Philosophie et les expériences naturelles.* The Hague: Martinus Nijhoff, 1961.

963   Waldenfels, Bernhard. "Das Problem der Leiblichkeit bei Merleau-Ponty." *Philosophisches Jahrbuch,* vol. 75, 1967-1968, pp. 345-365.

964   Zaner, Richard M. "Merleau-Ponty's theory of the body-proper," pp. 127-238 in *The Problem of Embodiment. Some Contributions to a Phenomenology of the Body.* The Hague: Martinus Nijhoff, 1964.

965   Zaner, Richard M. "Merleau-Ponty's theory of the body-proper as *'être-au-monde'*." *Journal of Existentialism,* vol. VI, no. 21, Fall 1965, pp. 31-39.

BODY-SOUL

Berger, Carol Altekruse. "Merleau-Ponty on the relations of body and soul." See Dissertation (No. 261).

Besson, Françoise Gisèle. "La doctrine cartésienne des relations de l'âme et du corps à la lumière de la lecture qu'en donne Merleau-Ponty." See Dissertation (No. 262).

Cromp, Germaine. "Le rapport âme-corps chez le premier Marcel." See MARCEL (no. 816).

Delfino, R. *Cuerpo y alma en Merleau-Ponty*. See Books (No. 234).

966   Delfino, R. "Cuerpo y alma en Merleau-Ponty." *Ciencia y Fé*, vol. XX, 1964, pp. 35-76.

967   Deprun, Jean, (ed.). *L'Union de l'âme et du corps chez Malebranche, Biran et Bergson:* Notes prises au cours de Merleau-Ponty à l'Ecole Normale Supérieure (1947-1948). Paris: J. Vrin, 1968.

Lapointe, François H. "The body-soul dialectic in Merleau-Ponty's *Structure of Behavior*." See *Structure du Comportement* (No. 349).

968   Racette, Jean. "Le corps et l'âme, la chair et l'esprit selon Merleau-Ponty." *Dialogue*, vol. V, no. 3, Dec. 1966, pp. 346-359.

CAUSALITY

969   Bornheim, Gerd A. "Fenomenologia e causalidade em Merleau-Ponty." *Revista Brasileira de Filosofia*, vol. XIX, fasc. 75, July-Sept. 1969, pp. 305-333.

Gerber, Rudolph J. See ATHEISM (Nos. 928, 929).

CHIASMA

Boehm, R. See HEIDEGGER (No. 777).

COGITO

Busch, T. W. "The role of the cogito in the philosophy of Merleau-Ponty." See Dissertation (No. 269).

970   Derossi, Giorgio. "Tempo, soggetto, cogito e conoscenza intenzionale diretta (non-mediata) in Merleau-Ponty." *Filosofia* (Torino), vol. XV, 1964, pp. 687-715.

971 Isaza, Antonio. "Il cogito encarnado en Merleau-Ponty." *Franciscanum*, vol. XI, 1969, pp. 103-143, and *Ibid.*, pp. 265-301.

Jabbour, Victorine. "Descartes dans la philosophie de Merleau-Ponty, le 'cogito' et son interprétation phénoménologique." See Dissertation (No. 297).

COGNITION (Epistemology, knowledge)

972 Ballard, Edward G. "On cognition of the pre-cognitive: Merleau-Ponty." *Philosophical Quarterly*, vol. XI, no. 44, July 1961, pp. 238-244.

973 Blanco, Domingo. "Vida y conocimiento en la filosofía de Merleau-Ponty." *Revista de Filosofia*, vol. XX, 1961, pp. 177-195.

Cantwell, O. F. "Merleau-Ponty. Toward a phenomenological psychology of real knowledge." See Dissertation (No. 270).

Colin, P. "Phénoménologie et connaissance de Dieu." See GOD (No. 1089).

974 Francella, O. "Significado y alcance de lo naturalmente conocido frente a la gnoseologia contemporanea." *Sapientia*, vol. XXI, 1966, pp. 251-279.

Mallin, Samuel B. "Merleau-Ponty's metaphysical epistemology." See Dissertation (No. 308).

975 Shiner, Larry. "A phenomenological approach to historical knowledge." *History and Theory*, vol. VIII, no. 2, 1969, pp. 260-274.

Springer, W. C. See Dissertation (No. 331).

Szaszkiewicz, Jerzy. See French Books (No. 192).

COMMUNISM

976 Caute, David. *Communism and the French Intellectuals, 1914-1960.* London: André Deutsch, 1964, 413p. French trans. by Magdeleine Paz, *Le Communisme et les intellectuels français, 1914-1960.* Paris: Gallimard, 1967.

Châtelet, François. See *Les Aventures* (No. 475).

977 KAJ. "Mandaryni, komunizm, koegzystencja." *Kultura*, no. 9/95, Sept. 1955, pp. 132-142.

116   COMMUNISM

978   Martins, Diamantino. "O communismo existencialista de Maurice Merleau-Ponty." *Revista Portuguesa de Filosofia*, vol. IX, no. 3, July-Sept. 1953, pp. 225-230.

979   O'Brien, Conor Cruise. "Communists and '*communisants*'," pp. 81-84 in *Writers and Politics*. London: Chatto & Windus, 1965. 259p.

COMMUNICATION

980   Iser, Wolfgang. *The Implied Reader: Patterns of Communication in prose fiction*. Baltimore: The Johns Hopkins Press, 1974.

Lanigan, Richard L. "Speaking and semiology: Merleau-Ponty's phenomenological theory of existential communication." See Dissertation (No. 303).

Lanigan, Richard L. Speaking and semiology: Maurice Merleau-Ponty's phenomenological theory of existential communication. See Books (No. 146).

981   Lanigan, Richard L. "Merleau-Ponty's phenomenology of communication." *Philosophy Today*, vol. XIV, no. 2, Summer 1970, pp. 79-88.

982   Madinier, Gabriel. "Réflexions sur la notion de 'communication'," pp. 165-170 in *Vers une philosophie réflexive*. Préface d'Aimé Forest. Neuchâtel: Editions de la Baconnière, 1960. 170p.

Poole, Roger C. See LEVI-STRAUSS (No. 808).

Purdy, Michael W. "Communication and institution in the phenomenology of Merleau-Ponty." See Dissertation (No. 322).

CONCEPT

Bruzina, Ronald C. "Logos and eidos: A study in the phenomenological meaning of 'concept' according to Husserl and Merleau-Ponty." See Dissertation (No. 267).

983   Smith, Colin. "The concept as expression," pp. 114-136 in *Contemporary French Philosophy. A Study in Norms and Values*. London: Methuen & Co., 1964.

CONSCIOUSNESS

984 Bergeron, André. "La conscience engagée dans le régime des significations selon Merleau-Ponty." *Dialogue*, vol. V, no. 3, Dec. 1966, pp. 373-382.

985 Busch, T. W. "Consciousness and transcendental philosophy: A response to Professor Tibbetts." *Philosophy Today*, vol. XIV, no. 4, Winter 1970, pp. 299-304.

Carr, David. "Maurice Merleau-Ponty: Incarnate consciousness," pp. 369-429 in see General Presentation (No. 645).

986 Gerber, Rudolph J. "Merleau-Ponty: The dialectic of consciousness and world." *Man and World*, vol. II, no. 1, Feb. 1969, pp. 83-107.

987 Hanley, C. M. T. "Phenomenology, consciousness and freedom." *Dialogue*, vol. V, no. 3, Dec. 1966, pp. 323-345.

987a Masotta, O. *Conciencia y estructura*. Buenos Aires: J. Alvaréz, 1968.

987b Ruyer, Raymond. *Paradoxes de la conscience et limites de l'automatisme*. Paris: Albin Michel, 1966. 286p.

Schouwers, Pierre. See Dissertation (No. 329).

Struyker Boudier, C. E. M. See Books (No. 256).

988 Tibbetts, Paul. "The recall of consciousness from temporary exile." *Philosophy Today*, vol. XIV, no. 4, Winter 1970, pp. 293-299.

989 Tibbetts, Paul. "Some recent philosophical contributions to the problem of consciousness." *Philosophy Today*, vol. XIV, Spring 1970, pp. 3-22.

990 Tibbetts, Paul. "Some recent empirical contributions to the problem of consciousness." *Philosophy Today*, vol. XIV, Spring 1970, pp. 23-32.

CONTINGENCY

Fabian, Rainer. See Dissertation (No. 281).

Mayo, Stephan T. "Aftermath of the absolute. A study of contingency in the phenomenology of Merleau-Ponty." See Dissertation (No. 311).

CONTINGENCY

991   Pfeiffer, M. L. "La contingencia en Merleau-Ponty." *Stromata*, vol. XXIX, July-Sept. 1973, pp. 241-257.

Zeiler, Judith. See Dissertation (No. 339).

CREATION

992   Gavaert, J. "Attorno al paradigma della creazione." *Salesianum*, vol. XXIX, 1967, pp. 701-713.

CRITICISM

Donato, Eugenio. See STRUCTURALISM (No. 1355).

993   Doubrovsky, Serge. *Pourquoi la nouvelle critique? Critique et objectivité*. Paris: Mercure de France, 1969. English Trans. by Derek Callman, *The New Criticism*. Chicago: University of Chicago Press, 1973.

CULTURE (and Cultural Studies)

Taylor, Darrell. See Dissertation (No. 334).

DESIRE

994   Lapointe, François H. "The phenomenology of desire and love in Merleau-Ponty." *Journal of Phenomenological Psychology*, vol. IV, no. 2, Spring 1974, pp. 445-459.

DEVELOPMENT (Includes Itinerary, Formation, Genesis)

995   Casalis, Mathieu. "Merleau-Ponty's philosophical itinerary: From phenomenology to onto-semiology." *The Southwestern Journal of Philosophy*, vol. VI, Winter 1975, pp. 63-69.

Geraets, Theodore. See Dissertation (No. 288).

Geraets, Theodore. See French Books (No. 196).

996   Friedman, Robert M. "The formation of Merleau-Ponty's philosophy." *Philosophy Today*, vol. XVII, Winter 1973, pp. 272-278.

Good, Paul. See Dissertation (No. 290).

997   Goyard, Pierre. "L'itinéraire politique de Maurice Merleau-Ponty." *Politique*, T. IX, nos. 33-36, 1966, pp. 273-319.

998 Green, André. "Du comportement à la chair: itinéraire de Merleau-Ponty." *Critique*, vol. XX, no. 211, décembre 1964, pp. 1017-1042.

999 Hyppolite, Jean. "L'évolution de la pensée de Merleau-Ponty," pp. 705-730 in vol. 2, *Figures de la pensée philosophique. Ecrits (1931-1968)*. Paris: Presses Universitaires de France, 1971.

1000 Kwant, Remy C. "De ontwikkeling van Merleau-Ponty's denken." *Tijdschrift voor Filosofie*, vol. XXVI, 1964, pp. 627-670.

Lacroix, Jean. "L'itinéraire de Merleau-Ponty." *Le Monde*, May 6, 1961, p. 9.

DIALECTIC (see also *Les Aventures de la dialectique*)

Barilli, R. "Merleau-Ponty e l'iperdialettica," pp. 204-239, see AESTHETIC (No. 889).

Gerber, Rudolph J. See CONSCIOUSNESS (No. 986).

1001 Hyppolite, Jean. "Existence et dialectique dans la philosophie de Merleau-Ponty." *Les Temps Modernes*, 17e année, nos. 184-185, octobre-novembre 1961, pp. 228-244. Also in *Cultura Universitaria*, nos. 78-79, 1962, pp. 92-104. Reprinted pp. 685-704 in *Figures de la pensée philosophique. Ecrits (1931-1968)*. Paris: Presses Universitaires de France, 1971. 2 vols.

1002 Lefebvre, Henri. "Les dilemmes de la dialectique." *Mediations*, no. 2, 1961, pp. 79-105.

Murphy, Richard T. See Dissertation (No. 319).

Ollero Tassara, Andrés. *Dialectica y praxis en Merleau-Ponty*. See Books (No. 241).

Paci, Enzo. Merleau-Ponty, Lukács, e il problema della dialettica. See LUKACS (No. 813).

Sandrini, F. "La fenomenología di Merleau-Ponty e il rapporto dialettico." See Dissertation (No. 327).

DIALOGUE

1003 Jolif, J. Y. "M. Merleau-Ponty ou la vertu du dialogue." *Economie et Humanisme*, vol. XX, 1961, pp. 10-12.

DUALISM

DUALISM of mind

1004 Yolton, John. "The dualism of mind." *The Journal of Philosophy*, vol. LI, no. 6, March 18, 1954, pp. 173-180.

ECONOMIC

1005 Bien, Joseph. "Man and the economic: Merleau-Ponty's interpretation of historical materialism." *Southwestern Journal of Philosophy*, vol. III, no. 1, 1972, pp. 121-127.

EDUCATION

Palermo, James. See No. 1289a.

ENCOUNTER

1006 Kwant, Remy C. *Wijsbegeerte van de ontmoeting*. Utrecht, 1959. English trans. by Henry Koren, *Encounter*. Pittsburgh: Duquesne University Press, 1960.

EPISTEMOLOGY

See COGNITION.

EROS

1007 Farrell Krell, David. "Maurice Merleau-Ponty on *Eros* and *Logos*." *Man and World*, vol. VII, no. 2, Feb. 1974, pp. 37-52.

ESSENTIALISM

Smith, Colin. "Sartre and Merleau-Ponty: The case for a modified essentialism." See SARTRE (No. 861).

ETHICS

Arras, John Dyer. "A criticism of existentialist ethics." See Dissertation (No. 259).

1008 Aufranc, D. M. "La visión del hombre y su sentido ético a través de la filosofía de Merleau-Ponty." *Universidad* (Argentina), vol. 70, 1967, pp. 21-42.

1009 Christoff, Daniel. "La tâche d'une morale philosophique." *Revue de Théologie et de Philosophie*, 3e série, tome 2, no. 2, 1952, pp. 107-119.

1010   Edie, James M. Review of Olafson, F. A., *Principles and Persons*. *Journal of Philosophy*, vol. LXV, 1968, pp. 456-462.

1011   Fuss, Peter. Review of Olafson, *Principles and Persons*. *Journal of the History of Philosophy*, vol. IX, April 1971, pp. 274-277.

1012   Hamrick, William S. See WHITEHEAD (No. 878).

1013   Lukács, Georg. "L'éthique existentialiste et la responsabilité historique," pp. 198-252, in *Existentialisme ou marxisme?* Paris: Nagel, 1948.

1014   Manser, A. R. "Existence and ethics," pp. 11-26 in *The Aristotelian Society. Supplementary volume 37*, 1963. Published for the Aristotelian Society by Harrison & Sons, Ltd., 1963, 216p.

1015   Olafson, Frederick A. *Principles and Persons. An Ethical Interpretation of Existentialism*. Baltimore: The Johns Hopkins Press, 1967.

1016   Pompei, Paolo. "Merleau-Ponty, politica e morale." *Il Verri*, vol. V, no. 6, Dec. 1961, pp. 144-156.

Somerville, John. See HUMANISME (No. 451).

1017   Santoni, R. E. "*Principles and Persons*, by Frederick A. Olafson." *International Philosophical Quarterly*, vol. IX, 1969, pp. 141-145.

Schouwers, Pierre E. See Dissertation (No. 329).

1018   Wild, John D. "Authentic existence." *Ethics*, vol. LXV, no. 4, July 1955, pp. 227-239.

1019   Wyss, Dieter. *Strukturen den Moral Untersuchungen zur Anthropologie und Genealogie moralischer Verhaltensweisen*. Göttingen: Vandenhoeck & Ruprecht, 1968.

EXISTENCE

Hyppolite, Jean. See DIALECTIQUE (No. 1001).

Hyppolite, Jean. *Sens et existence dans la philosophie de Maurice Merleau-Ponty*. See French Books (No. 184).

1020   Wahl, Jean. "Freedom and existence in some recent philosophies." *Philosophy and Phenomenological Research*, vol. VIII, no. 4, June 1948, pp. 539-556.

122   EXISTENCE

1021   Wild, John. "Contemporary phenomenology and the problem of existence." *Philosophy and Phenomenological Research*, vol. XX, 1959, pp. 166-180.

1022   Doubrovsky, J. J. "Existence and symbol." *Philosophy and Phenomenological Research*, vol. XXI, 1960, pp. 229-238.

EXISTENTIALISM

1023   Anonymous. "Merleau-Ponty, fenomenologo existencialista." *Filosofia*, 1958, pp. 291-293.

1024   Abbagnano, Nicolà. "Outline of a philosophy of existence." *Philosophy and Phenomenological Research*, vol. IX, 1948, pp. 200-211.

1025   Acton, H. B. "Philosophical survey: Philosophy in France." *Philosophy*, vol. XXIV, no. 88, Jan. 1949, pp. 77-81.

1026   Alquié, Ferdinand. "Une philosophie de l'ambiguité: l'existentialisme de Maurice Merleau-Ponty." *Fontaine*, vol. XI, no. 59, avril 1947, pp. 47-70.

1027   Ballanti, Graziella. "L'esistenzialismo di Maurice Merleau-Ponty." *Rivista di Filosofia Neo-Scolastica*, vol. 44, no. 5, Sept.-Oct. 1952, pp. 458-461.

1028   Bayer, Raymond. "Merleau-Ponty's existentialism." *University of Buffalo Studies* (Monographs in Philosophy), vol. XIX, no. 3, 1951, pp. 95-104.

1029   Bayer, Raymond. "Merleau-Ponty et l'existentialisme." *Revue Philosophique de la France et de l'Etranger*, vol. 87, Jan.-March 1962, pp. 107-117.

       Bettler, Alan R.   See Dissertation (No. 265).

1030   Bruch, Jean-Louis. "L'existentialisme de Merleau-Ponty." *Conjonctions*, no. 75, janvier-mars 1959, pp. 8-10.

1031   Bubner, R. "Kritische Fragen zum Ende des französischen Existentialismus." *Philosophische Rundschau*, vol. XIV, 1967, pp. 241-257.

1032   Challaye, Félicien. "Immortalité et existentialisme." *Synthèses*, 11e année, no. 138, Jan. 1957, pp. 286-296.

1033   Chiodi, Pietro. *Il Pensiero esistenzialista*. Milano: Garzanti, 1959.

1034　Cuvillier, Armand. "De l'existentialisme au nazisme." *Revue Socialiste*, no. 4, octobre 1946, pp. 450-460.

1035　Daniélou, Jean. *Dialogue avec les existentialistes*, pp. 105-112. Paris: Le Portulan, 1948.

1036　Dufrenne, Mikel. "Existentialism and existentialisms." *Philosophy and Phenomenological Research*, vol. XXVI, no. 1, Sept. 1965, pp. 51-62.

1037　Earle, William. "Phenomenology and existentialism." *Journal of Philosophy*, vol. LVII, no. 2, Jan. 21, 1960, pp. 75-84.

　　　Fragata, Julio. See HUSSERL (No. 784).

1038　Grégoire, François. *Questions concernant l'existentialisme*. Louvain: Publications Universitaires de Louvain, 1951.

1039　Honingsheim, P. "Existentialismus und Volkerannaherung." *Friedens-Warte*, vol. LVI, 1961, pp. 34-42.

1040　Hyppolite, Jean. "A chronology of French existentialism." *Yale French Studies*, no. 16, Winter 1955-1956, pp. 100-102.

1041　Jeanson, Francis. "Situation de l'existentialisme." *La Gazette des Lettres*, 7e année, no. 14, 15 novembre 1951, pp. 31-36.

1042　Kingston, F. Temple. "An introduction to existentialist thought." *The Dalhousie Review*, vol. 40, no. 2, Summer 1960, pp. 181-188.

1043　Kingston, F. Temple. *French Existentialism. A Christian Critique*. Toronto: University of Toronto Press, 1961.

1044　Langan, Thomas. "Existentialism and phenomenology in France," pp. 374-408 in Etienne Gilson, et al. (eds.), *Recent Philosophy. Hegel to the Present*. New York: Random House, 1966.

1045　Lessing, Arthur. "Marxist existentialism." *Review of Metaphysics*, vol. XX, 1967, pp. 461-482.

1046　Lotthe, Etienne. "Modern French philosophy." *Circle Magazine*, no. 1, Jan. 1964, pp. 6-9.

EXISTENTIALISM

1047 Meyer, Rudolf W. "Maurice Merleau-Ponty und das Schicksal des französischen Existentialismus." *Philosophische Rundschau*, vol. V, nos. 3-4, 1955, pp. 129-165.

1048 Mougin, Henri. *La sainte famille existentialiste*. Paris: Editions Sociales, 1947.

1049 Morot-Sir, Edouard. "La critique existentialiste, 3. Maurice Merleau-Ponty," pp. 34-38 in *La Pensée française d'aujourd'hui*. Paris: Presses Universitaires de France, 1971.

1050 Passmore, John. "Existentialism and phenomenology," pp. 466-503 in *A Hundred Years of Philosophy*. Harmondsworth, Middlesex: Penguin Books, 1968, 639p.

1051 Puente, Ojea G. "Existencialismo y marxismo en el pensamiento de Merleau-Ponty." *Cuadernos Hispanoamericanos*, no. 30, 1957, pp. 41-88.

Ram Adhar Mall. "Existentialism as philosophical anthropology." See ANTHROPOLOGY (No. 919).

Rice, Philip. See SELF (No. 1343).

1052 Sciacca, Michele Federico. "L'esistenzialismo," pp. 400-404 in *La Filosofia oggi*, vol. II. Milano: Marzorati, 1958.

1053 Semerari, Giuseppe. "Esistenzialismo e marxismo nella *Fenomenologia della percezione*." (See Nos. 468 and 469.)

Spiegelberg, Herbert. "Husserl's phenomenology and existentialism." See HUSSERL (No. 794).

1054 Spiegelberg, Herbert. "French existentialism: Its social philosophy." *Kenyon Review*, vol. XVI, no. 3, Summer 1954, pp. 446-462.

1055 Symposium. "Existentialist thought and contemporary philosophy in the West." *Journal of Philosophy*, vol. LIII, Nov. 1956, pp. 739-771.

1056 Tilliette, Xavier. "Merleau-Pontys Philosophie der Endlichkeit." *Dokumente*, vol. XVII, 1961, pp. 271-282.

Truc, Gonzague. "L'existentialisme au Collège de France." See ELOGE (No. 599).

1057   Urango, E. "Maurice Merleau-Ponty: fenomenologia y existencialismo." *Filosofia y Letras*, vol. XV, no. 30, 1948, pp. 219-242.

1058   Valentini, Francesco. "Esistenzialismo e marxismo: Rassegna di scritti francese." *Giornale Critico della Filosofia Italiana*, vol. XXXI, Jan.-March 1952, pp. 78-96.

1059   Viano, Carlo A. "Esistenzialismo ed umanesimo in Maurice Merleau-Ponty." *Rivista di Filosofia*, vol. 44, no. 1, Jan. 1953, pp. 38-60.

1060   Waelhens, Alphonse de. "De la phénoménologie à l'existentialisme," in *Le Choix, le monde, l'existence*. (Cahiers du Collège Philosophique). Paris: Arthaud, 1947.

1061   Waelhens, Alphonse de. "La filosofia politica del marxismo e del esistenzialismo: Merleau-Ponty." *Delta*, nuova serie, no. 4, 1953, pp. 21-40.

1062   Wahl, Jean. "Brève introduction aux philosophies françaises de l'existence." *Encyclopédie Française: Philosophie-Religion*, vol. XIX, 12. pp. 3-8. Paris: Librairie Larousse, 1957.

1063   Wahl, Jean. "A propos d'une conférence de M. Merleau-Ponty sur les aspects politiques et sociaux de l'existentialisme." *Fontaine*, vol. V, 1946, pp. 678-679.

1064   Wild, John. "Existentialism as a philosophy." *Journal of Philosophy*, vol. LVII, no. 2, Jan. 21, 1960, pp. 45-62.

1065   Winthroop, Henry. "Existential and phenomenological frontiers." *Journal of Existentialism*, vol. VI, 1966, pp. 459-486.

1066   Zaner, Richard M. "Existentialism as a logos of man. The case of M. Merleau-Ponty." *Memorias del XXXIII Congresso Internacional de Filosofia*, V, (Sept. 7-14, 1963), pp. 409-421. Reprinted in book form, Vol. V: *Communicaciones libras*. Mexico: Universidad Nacional Autonoma de Mexico, 1964.

EXISTENTIALISM AND MARXISM

1067   Duvignaud, Jean. "Der marxistisch-existentialistische Disput," pp. 39-46 in *Französische Kultur 1962*. Köln: Verlag der Dokumente, 1962. 112p.

EXISTENTIALISM AND MARXISM

1068   Kuhn, H. "Existentialism und Marxismus. Zu Merleau-Pontys Philosophie der Zweideutigkeit." *Philosophisches Jahrbuch*, vol. LXII, 1953, pp. 327-343.

1069   Lessing, Arthur. "Marxist existentialism." *Review of Metaphysics*, vol. XX, 1967, pp. 461-482.

Semerari, Giuseppe. See PHEN (Nos. 408 and 409).

EXPERIENCE

1070   Herbenick, Raymond. "On speaking of experience: Merleau-Ponty's conceptual model." *University of Dayton Review*, vol. VIII, no. 1, Summer 1971, pp. 65-91.

Tibbetts, Paul. "William James and the doctrine of 'pure experience'." See JAMES (No. 799).

1071   Tibbets, Paul. "The 'levels of experience' doctrine in modern philosophy." *Studi Internazionali di Filosofia*, vol. III, Autumn 1971, pp. 15-32.

EXPRESSION

1072   Cowley, Fraser. "L'expression et la parole d'après Merleau-Ponty." *Dialogue*, vol. V, no. 3, Dec. 1966, pp. 360-372.

1073   Edie, James M. "Expression and metaphor." *Philosophy and Phenomenological Research*, vol. XXIII, no. 4, June 1963, pp. 538-561.

Kwant, Remy C. *Mens en expressie in het licht van de wijsbegeerte van Merleau-Ponty*. See Dutch Books (No. 254).

1074   Kwant, Remy C. *The Phenomenology of Expression*. Pittsburgh: Duquesne University Press, 1970.

1075   Natanson, Maurice. "The fabric of expression." *Review of Metaphysics*, vol. XXI, no. 3, issue no. 82, March 1968, pp. 491-504.

Park, Ynhui. "An ontological interpretation of the concept of expression in the philosophy of Merleau-Ponty." See Dissertation (No. 318).

1075a   Schwartzmann, Felix. *Teoria de la Expresión*. Santiago: Universidad de Chili, 1965.

FAITH (see also religion)

1076 Dondeyne, Albert. *Foi chrétienne et pensée contemporaine.* Louvain, 1952. Revised English trans, *Contemporary European Thought and Christian Faith.* Pittsburgh: Duquesne University Press, 4th ed., 1968.

1077 Duméry, Henry. *La foi n'est pas un cri.* Paris: Castermann, 1957.

FASCINATION

Hamrick, William S. See PORNOGRAPHY (No. 1318).

FLESH (see also body)

1078 Frantz, John J. "Merleau-Ponty's notion of flesh: A look at the development of a new philosophical insight." *Dialogue,* Journal of Phi Sigma Tau. National Honor Society for Philosophy, vol. XIV, Jan. 1972, pp. 46-51.

1079 Gillan, Garth. "Toward the foundations of hermeneutics: The signifying flesh." *Philosophy Today,* vol. XVI, no. 1, Spring 1972, pp. 4-11.

1080 Lefort, Claude. "Le corps, la chair." *L'Arc,* no. 46, 1971, pp. 5-18.

Racette, Jean. See BODY (No. 968).

FOR-ITSELF & IN-ITSELF

Moreland, John M. See SARTRE (No. 851).

FORM

Hartley, John J. See Dissertation (No. 292).

FREEDOM

1081 Cristaldi, Mariano. *Libertà e metafisica.* Bologna: Casa Editrice Prof. Riccardo Patron, 1964, chapter 3, pp. 61-69, 13-44.

Gahamanyi, Célestin. See Dissertation (No. 286).

Hanley, C. M.T. See CONSCIOUSNESS (No. 987).

King, Thomas W. See Dissertation (No. 301).

McCleary, Richard C. See Dissertation (No. 312).

FREEDOM

1082 Naville, Pierre. *Les Conditions de la liberté.* Paris: Sagittaire, 1947.

1083 Papi, Fulvio. "Libertà e marxismo in Merleau-Ponty," *Atti del XII Congresso Internazionale di Filosofia,* 1958, vol. XII, pp. 361-368. *Storia della filosofia moderna e contemporanea.* Firenze: Sansoni, 1961.

Wahl, Jean. See EXISTENCE (No. 1020).

GENEVE (Recontres Internationales)

1084 Spender, Stephen. "Meeting at Geneva." *Time & Tide,* vol. XXVII, no. 42, Oct. 19, 1946, pp. 996-998.

1085 Thévenaz, Pierre. "Les VIe rencontres internationales de Genève: La connaissance de l'homme au XXE siècle." *Revue de Théologie et de Philosophie,* 3e série, tome I, no. III, 1951, pp. 221-224.

GENESIS

Holenstein, E. See HUSSERL 1971 and 1972 (Nos. 786 and 787).

GERMANY

1086 Biemel, Walter. "Sartres Widerpart: Maurice Merleau-Ponty in Deutschland." *Die Zeit,* vol. XXI, no. 42, 1966, p. 29.

GESTALT THEORY

1087 Dillon, Martin C. "Gestalt theory and Merleau-Ponty's concept of intentionality." *Man and World,* vol. IV, Nov. 1971, pp. 436-459.

Reboul, Olivier. "Imaginer et percevoir: Alain, la Gestaltthéorie et Merleau-Ponty," pp. 106-114, in ALAIN (No. 756).

GOD (see also absolute, atheism, faith, religion)

1088 Bannan, John F. "Merleau-Ponty on God." *International Philosophical Quarterly,* vol. VI, no. 3, Sept. 1966, pp. 341-365.

1089 Colin, Pierre. "Phénoménologie et connaissance de Dieu." *Recherches de Philosophie,* 1958. Whole issue is devoted to the problem "De la connaissance de Dieu," pp. 299-405.

1090 Sanabria, José Ruben. *Filosofía del absoluto. Affirmación y rechazo de Dios en diversas corrientes filosóficas.* México, DF.: Editorial Progresso, 1966.

Touron del Pie, Eliseo. See Spanish Books (No. 245).

1091 Vandenbussche, Franz. "Het Godsprobleem in de filosofie van Merleau-Ponty." *Bijdragen*, vol. XXVIII, no. 1, Supplement 1967, pp. 63-81.

1092 Vandenbussche, Franz. "Les approches du problème de Dieu dans la philosophie de Merleau-Ponty." *De Deo in Philosophia S. Thomae et in hodierna philosophia*, vol. 2, pp. 339-344. (Acta, VI Congressus Thomistici Internationalis). Romae: Officium Libri Catholici, 1966.

1093 Vandenbussche, Franz. "The problem of God in the philosophy of Merleau-Ponty." *International Philosophical Quarterly*, vol. VII, no. 1, March 1967, pp. 45-67.

GRAMMAR

1094 Edie, James M. "Can Grammar be thought?" pp. 315-345 in James M. Edie, Francis H. Parker, Calvin O. Schrag, eds., *Patterns of the Life-world. Essays in Honor of John Wild.* Evanston, Ill.: Northwestern University Press, 1970.

HERMENEUTICS

Gillan, Garth. See FLESH (No. 1079).

HISTORY

Albert, Hughes. "Histoire et historicité chez Merleau-Ponty." See Dissertation (No. 258).

1095 Bakker, Reinout. "De geschiedenis in het denken van Merleau-Ponty." *Wijsgerig Perspectief op Maatschappij en Wetenschapp*, vol. VI, 1965-1966, pp. 44-56.

Bien, Joseph. "Merleau-Ponty's conception of history," pp. 127-142 in Gillan Books (No. 135).

1095a Bien, Joseph. "Man and the economic: Merleau-Ponty's interpretation of historical materialism." *The Southwestern Journal of Philosophy*, vol. III, no. 1, 1972, pp. 121-127.

130   HISTORY

1096   Bonomi, Andrea. "Materialismo storico e questione
        esistenziale." *Aut Aut*, no. 75, 1963, pp. 66-73.

1097   Buonajuto, M. "Esistenza e storia." *Ricerche
        Filosofiche*, vol. XXXI, 1963, pp. 4-14.

        Caillois, Roland. See No. 370.

1098   Caillois, Roland. "Le monde vécu et l'histoire,"
        pp. 7-24, in *L'Homme, le monde, l'histoire*.
        Paris: Arthaud, 1948.

        Caillois, Roland. See ELOGE (No. 581).

        Centineo, Ettore. *Una fenomenologia della storia*.
        See Italian Books (No. 222).

        Debray, Régis. ARTS (No. 802). See SIGNES (No. 516).

        Fabian, Rainer. See Dissertation (No. 281).

        Ibañez Martín Mellado, José Antonio. See Spanish
        Books (No. 239).

1097   Kwant, Remy C. "Menselijke existencie en geschiedenis
        volgens het wijsgerig denken von Maurice Merleau-
        Ponty." *Algemeen Nederlands Tijdschrift voor
        Wijsbegeerte en Psychologie*, 1954, pp. 230-247.
        [Summary in French.]

1098   Kwant, Remy C. "De historie en het absolute. Kri-
        tische analyse van de opvatting van Merleau-
        Ponty." *Tijdschrift voor Filosofie*, vol. XVII,
        1955, pp. 255-304. [Summary in French.]

1099   Lagueux, Maurice. "Y a-t-il une philosophie de
        l'histoire chez Merleau-Ponty?" *Dialogue*, vol.
        V, no. 3, Dec. 1966, pp. 404-417.

        Lukács, Georg. See ETHICS (No. 1013).

        Matukanga, Boniface. "Merleau-Ponty et l'histoire
        de son temps." See Dissertation (No. 310).

1100   Muglioni, J. "L'histoire et la vérité." *Revue
        Socialiste*, no. 90, 1955, pp. 312-321.

1101   Olafson, Frederick A. "Existentialism, Marxism and
        historical justification." *Ethics*, vol. LXV, no.
        2, Jan. 1965, pp. 126-134.

1102   O'Neill, John. "Perception, expression and history
        in the philosophy of Merleau-Ponty." *Social Re-
        search*, vol. XXXIV, Spring 1967, pp. 47-66.

O'Neill, John. See Books English (No. 153).

1103 Pax, Clyde. "Merleau-Ponty and the truth of history." *Man and World*, vol. VI, Sept. 1973, pp. 270-279.

Shiner, Larry. "A phenomenological approach to historical knowledge," see COGNITION (No. 975).

1104 Truc, Gonzague. "L'homme et l'histoire." *Hommes-Mondes*, vol. IX, 1954, pp. 243-248.

Walter, Emil H. See HABERMAS (No. 775).

HOPE

Zeiler, Judith. See Dissertation (No. 339).

IDEALISM

1105 Desanti, Jean-T. "Merleau-Ponty et la décomposition de l'idéalisme." *La Nouvelle Critique*, vol. IV, no. 37, juin 1952, pp. 63-82.

Devaux, André. See MOREAU (No. 822).

IDEOLOGY

1106 Siméon, Jean-Paul. "Vérité et idéologie. La critique de la théorie des idéologies dans les premières oeuvres de Merleau-Ponty." *L'Arc*, no. 46, 1971, pp. 48-55.

IMAGINATION

1107 Theobald, David W. "The imagination and what philosophers have to say." *Diogenes*, no. 57, Spring 1967, pp. 47-63.

IMAGINING (and perceiving)

Reboul, Olivier. See ALAIN (No. 756).

IMMORTALITY

Challaye, Félicien. See EXISTENTIALISM (No. 312).

IN-DER-WELT-SEIN

Podlech, Adalbert. See German Books (No. 209).

1108 Toscano, Giuseppe. "l' 'In-der-Welt-Sein' di Maurice Merleau-Ponty." *Teorisi*, vol. XIX, nos. 3-4, July-Dec. 1964, pp. 149-223.

INDIVIDUAL

Lorenz, Hélène S. "Hierarchic man: Philosophy and the individual in the work of Merleau-Ponty." See Dissertations (No. 304).

IN MEMORIAM

1109 Alquié, Ferdinand. "Maurice Merleau-Ponty." *Cahiers du Sud*, vol. 48, nos. 362-363, Sept.-Nov. 1961, pp. 153-155.

1110 Audry, Colette. "La vie d'un philosophie. In Memoriam." *L'Express*, 11 mai 1961, no. 517, pp. 35-37.

1111 Bataillon, Marcel. "Eloge prononcé devant l'Assemblée des Professeurs du Collège de France, 25 juin 1961." *Annuaire du Collège de France*, pp. 37-40. Paris: Imprimerie Nationale, 1961.

1112 Brusch, Jean-Louis. "Maurice Merleau-Ponty." *Marginales*, vol. XVI, nos. 80-81, novembre-decembre 1961, pp. 60-62.

1113 Cascales, Charles. "M. Merleau-Ponty philosophe de l'engagement." *Convivium*, nos. 11-12, 1961, pp. 45-74.

1114 Deguy, Michel. "Maurice Merleau-Ponty." *Preuves*, no. 124, juin 1961, pp. 60-62.

1115 Deguy, Michel. "Hommage à Merleau-Ponty: In Memoriam." *La Nouvelle Revue Française*, vol. IX, no. 102, ier juin 1961, pp. 1118-1120.

1116 Dufrenne, Mikel. "Maurice Merleau-Ponty." *Les Etudes Philosophiques*, vol. XVII, no. 1, janvier-mars 1962, pp. 81-92. Reprinted in *Jalons*, pp. 208-221. The Hague: Martinus Nijhoff, 1966.

1117 Duvignaud, Jean. "Merleau-Ponty, une méditation interrompue." *Tendances*, no. 11-12, juin-août 1961, pp. 433-440.

1118 Galindez, J. "M. Merleau-Ponty." *Humanitas*, vol. IX, no. 14, 1961, pp. 288-289.

1119 Gandillac, Maurice de. "Maurice Merleau-Ponty. In Memoriam." *Revue Philosophique de la France et de l'Etranger*, vol. 87, janvier-mars, 1962, pp. 103-106.

1120 Kwant, Remy C. "Levensechte wijsbegeerte. Naar aanleiding van de dood van Maurice Merleau-Ponty." *Gawein, Tijdschrift voor Psychologie*, vol. X, 1961, pp. 71-81.

1121 Kwant, Remy C. "O.E.S.A. In Memoriam M. Merleau-Ponty." *Streven*, vol. XIV, 1960-1961, pp. 946-960.

1122 Lacroix, Jean. "L'itinéraire de Merleau-Ponty." *Le Monde*, 6 mai 1961, p. 9.

1123 Langan, Thomas. "Maurice Merleau-Ponty. In Memoriam." *Philosophy and Phenomenological Research*, vol. XXIII, no. 3, Dec. 1962, pp. 205-216.

1124 Lefort, Claude. "M. Merleau-Ponty..." *Le Figaro Littéraire*, vol. XVI, no. 786, 13 mai 1961, p. 13.

1125 Piantier, J. "Maurice Merleau-Ponty est mort." *Le Monde*, 5 mai 1961, p. 1.

1126 Ricoeur, Paul. "Le philosophe foudroyé." *Les Nouvelles Littéraires*, no. 1758, 11 mai 1961, p. 4. Reprinted in *Christianisme Social*, vol. 69, 1961, pp. 389-395.

1127 Ricoeur, Paul. "Hommage à Merleau-Ponty." *Esprit*, vol. XXIX, juin 1961, pp. 1115-1120.

1128 Tilliette, Xavier. "Une philosophie sans absolu: Maurice Merleau-Ponty 1908-1961." *Etudes*, tome 305, septembre 1961, pp. 215-229.

1129 Van Haecht, Louis. "In Memoriam. Maurice Merleau-Ponty (1908-1961)." *Dietsche Warande en Belfort*, vol. 106, 1961, pp. 272-274.

1130 Vita, Luis Washington. "Maurice Merleau-Ponty (1908-1961). In Memoriam." *Revista Brasileira de Filosofia*, vol. XI, 1961, pp. 272-274.

1131 Vita, Luis Washington. "Tambien os filosofos morrem... (M. Merleau-Ponty, 1908-1961)," pp. 67-76, in *Monologos y dialogos* (Colecao Ensayo). Sao Paulo Conselho Estadual de Cultura, Comissao de Literatura. Sao Paulo, 1964. 164p.

1132 Waelhens, Alphonse de. "In Memoriam. Maurice Merleau-Ponty." *Tijdschrift voor Filosofie*, vol. XXIII, no. 2, June 1961, pp. 340-347.

1133 Waelhens, Alphonse de. "Maurice Merleau-Ponty." *Revue Philosophique de Louvain*, vol. LIX, mai 1961, pp. 378-380.

Waelhens, Alphonse de. "Situations de Merleau-Ponty," see General Presentation (No. 745).

1134 Waelhens, Alphonse de. "Maurice Merleau-Ponty." *Revista Portuguesa de Filosofia*, vol. XVIII, 1962, pp. 176-184.

1135 Wahl, Jean. "Cette pensée. . . ." *Les Temps Modernes*, 17e année, nos. 184-185, octobre-novembre 1961, pp. 399-436.

INTENTIONALITY

Dillon, Martin C. See GESTALT THEORY (No. 1087).

1136 Hoorn, William L. van. "The development of the concept of intentionality." Psychologisch Instituut van de Rijksuniversiteit te Leiden. Rapport No. H 007-69.

Manniello, Andrew. See Dissertation (No. 309).

1137 Mohanty, J. N. *The Concept of Intentionality*. St. Louis: Warren T. Green, 1972.

1138 Mohanty, J. N. "Husserl on intentionality," in *Analecta Husserliana*, vol. I, ed. by A.-T. Tymieniecka. Dordrecht: D. Reidel Pub. Co., 1971.

1138a O'Connor, Tony. "Behavior and perception: A discussion of Merleau-Ponty's problem of operative intentionality." *Human Context-Le Domaine Humain*, vol. VII, Spring 1975, pp. 39-47.

1139 Olafson, Frederick A. "A central theme of Merleau-Ponty's philosophy," pp. 179-205 in Edward N. Lee & Maurice Mandelbaum, eds., *Phenomenology and Existentialism*. Baltimore: Johns Hopkins Press, 1967.

Rauch, Leo. "Intentionality and its development in the phenomenological psychology of Edmund Husserl." See Dissertation (No. 325).

INTERIORITY

1140 Borne, Etienne. "Pour une doctrine de l'intériorité," pp. 9-74 in *Intériorité et vie spirituelle* in *Recherches et débats* du Centre catholique des intellectuels français, nouvelle série, Cahier no. 7, avril 1954.

1141 Bouet, Michel M. "Le problème de l'intériorité objective dans la psychologie phénoménologique de Merleau-Ponty." *Les Etudes Philosophiques*, vol. III, nos. 3-4, juillet-décembre 1948, pp. 297-314.

INTERROGATION

1142 Derossi, Giorgio. "La struttura dell'interrogazione." *Archivio di Filosofia*, vol. XIX, 1968, pp. 75-102.

INTERSUBJECTIVITY (see also: The Other)

Cunningham, Suzanne M. See Dissertation (No. 274).

1143 Friedman, Robert M. "Merleau-ponty's theory of subjectivity (sic)." *Philosophy Today*, vol. XIX, no. 3, Fall 1975, pp. 228-242.

King, Thomas W. See Dissertation, FREEDOM (No. 301).

INTERVIEW

1144 Chapsal, Madeleine. "Maurice Merleau-Ponty," pp. 193-212, in *Les écrivains en personne*. Paris: René Julliard, 1960. 251p.

ITINERARY of M-P.

See DEVELOPMENT.

JUSTICE

Scarpelli, U. See MARXISM (No. 1227).

JUSTIFICATION

Monnerot, Jules. See HUMANISME (Nos. 442, 443, and 444).

Olafson, Frederick A. See HISTORY (No. 1101).

KANTIAN SCHEMATISM

Negri, A. See KANT (No. 800).

KNOWLEDGE

KNOWLEDGE

See COGNITION.

LANGUAGE (includes discours, parole, speech, word)

Barilli, R. See AESTHETICS (No. 889).

1145   Blanchot, Maurice. "Le 'discours philosophique'." *L'Arc*, no. 46, 1971, pp. 1-4.

1146   Brus, B. Th. "De taal bij Merleau-Ponty." *Nederlands Tijdschrift voor Psychologie*, vol. XIII, 1958, pp. 268-280.

1147   Brus, B. Th. "Een samenvatting van de zienswijzen van Maurice Merleau-Ponty met betrekking tot de taal." *Algemeen Nederlands Tijdschrift voor Wijsbegeerte Psychologie*, vol. LVI, 1963-1964, pp. 75-87.

1148   Capra, Silvio. "Il problema del linguaggio in Merleau-Ponty." *Rivista di Filosofia Neo-Scolastica*, anno 64, no. 3, July-Sept. 1972, pp. 446-470.

1149   Caramella, S. "Il languaggio ultraesistenziale di Merleau-Ponty." *Il Baretti*, May-Aug. 1961, pp. 27-36.

1146   Castilla Lázaro, Ramón. "La filosofía del lenguaje de Merleau-Ponty." *Dialôgos* (Universidad de Puerto Rico), vol. VI, no. 15, April-June 1969, pp. 35-73.

1147   Castoriadis, Cornelius. "Le dicible et l'indicible." *L'Arc*, no. 46, 1971, pp. 67-79.

1148   Ceriotto, C. L. "Lenguage y reflexión según Merleau-Ponty." *Filosofía* (Mendoza), no. 29, 1964, pp. 50-58.

1149   Charlesworth, James H. "Reflections on Merleau-Ponty's phenomenological description of 'word'." *Philosophy and Phenomenological Research*, vol. XXX, June 1970, pp. 609-613.

Charron, Ghyslain. See Martinet 1 & 2 and Books (Nos. 168, 818 and 819).

Cowley, Fraser. See EXPRESSION (No. 1072).

Cunningham, Suzanne M. See Dissertation Husserl (No. 274).

Dallery, Robert Carleton. See Dissertation (No. 275).

1150 Daly, James. "Merleau-Ponty's concept of phenomenology of language." *St. Louis Quarterly*, vol. IV, 1966, pp. 325-342.

1151 Derida, Jacques. "La forme et le vouloir-dire. Note sur la phénoménologie du langage." *Revue Internationale de Philosophie*, vol. XXI, 1967, pp. 277-299.

1152 Donato, Eugenio. "Language, vision and phenomenology: Merleau-Ponty as a test case." *Modern Language Notes*, vol. 85, no. 6, Dec. 1970, pp. 803-814. Reprinted in Richard Macksey, ed., *Velocities of Change. Critical Essays from MLN*, pp. 292-303. Baltimore-London: Johns Hopkins Press, 1974.

1153 Donato, Eugenio. "The two languages of criticism," pp. 89-97, in Richard Macksey and Eugenio Donato, eds., *The Language of Criticism and the Sciences of Man: The Structuralist Controversy*. See STRUCTURALISM.

1154 Dorfles, G. "La parola come segno dell'ineffabile." *Aut Aut*, no. 66, Nov. 1961, pp. 559-562.

1155 Doubrovsky, Serge. "L'enracinement de la parole dans le corps." *Le Monde [des Livres]*, no. 7857, 18 avril 1970, p. 5.

Fontaine de Visscher, Lucie. See 171a.

Fontan, Pierre. See *Phénoménologie* (No. 381).

Froman, Wayne Jeffrey. See Dissertation (No. 285).

1156 Gillan, Garth. "The temporality of language and the symbolic." *Philosophy and Rhetoric*, vol. III, Winter 1969, pp. 13-39.

Gillan, Garth. "In the folds of the flesh: Philosophy and language," pp. 1-61, in Gillan Books (See No. 135).

1157 A. G. "Merleau-Ponty, *Consciousness and the Acquisition of Language*." (a review). See M-P Bibliography (No. 143).

1158 Ihde, Don. "Language and two phenomenologies." *Southern Journal of Philosophy*, vol. VIII, Winter 1970, pp. 399-408. Reprinted in Edward G. Ballard & Charles E. Scott, eds. *Martin Heidegger in Europe and America*. The Hague: Nijhoff, 1974.

Ihde, Don. "Singing the world: Language and perception," pp. 61-77 in Gillan Books (See No. 135).

1159   Ihde, Don. *Sense and Significance*. Pittsburgh: Duquesne University Press, 1973. [pp. 123-127, 163-170, 175-178 and passim]

1160   Kemp, Peter. "Merleau-Ponty's phenomenology of language." *Danish Yearbook of Philosophy*, vol. IV, 1967, pp. 7-11.

1161   Kockelmans, Joseph J. "Merleau-Ponty's phenomenology of language." *Review of Existential Psychology and Psychiatry*, vol. III, no. 1, Feb. 1963, pp. 39-82.

1162   Kockelmans, Joseph J. "Language, meaning, and eksistence," in F. J. Smith, ed., *Phenomenology in Perspective*. The Hague: Martinus Nijhoff, 1970.

1163   Kwant, Remy C. *Phenomenology of Language*. Pittsburgh: Duquesne University Press, 1965.

Lagueux, Maurice. See SAUSSURE (No. 866).

1164   Lagueux, Maurice. "Le discours philosophique selon Maurice Merleau-Ponty," in *La Philosophie et les philosophes*, tome II, ed. by Y. Lafrance and J. King-Farlow. Montreal-Paris-Tournai: Desclée de Brouwer; Montréal: Les Editions Bellarmin, 1973.

Lanigan, Richard L. See COMMUNICATION (Nos. 146, 303 and 981).

1165   Lapointe, François. "Merleau-Ponty's phenomenology of language and General Semantics." *Research in Education*, May 1974.

1166   Lapouge, Claude. "Concilier la philosophie du sujet et la linguistique." *Le Monde [des Livres]*. no. 7857, 18 avril 1970, p. 4.

1167   Lefebvre, Henri. *Le langage et la société*. Paris: Gallimard, 1966.

1168   Lewis, Philip E. "Merleau-Ponty and the phenomenology of language." *Yale French Studies*, nos. 36-37, 1964-1965, pp. 19-40. Reprinted in Jacques Ehrmann, ed., *Structuralism*, pp. 9-31. New York: Doubleday, Anchor Books, 1970.

Micha, René. See LITERATURE (No. 1202).

Nethold, Ana Maria, ed. See SAUSSURE (No. 867).

1169   O'Mahoney, Brendan E. "The rediscovery of language."
       Studies, LIII, Spring 1964, pp. 72-84.

       O'Neill, John. See LA PROSE (No. 619).

1170   Pochtar, Ricardo. "Experiencia del lenguaje y
       pasividad." *Cuadernos de Filosofía* (Buenos Aires),
       vol. IX, July-Dec. 1969, pp. 245-262.

1171   Pontalis, J.-B. "Présence, entre les signes,
       absence." *L'Arc*, no. 46, 1971, pp. 56-66.

1172   P.M.S. "M. Merleau-Ponty, Sur la phénoménologie du
       langage." *Revue Philosophique de la France et
       de l'Etranger*, vol. 77, 1952, pp. 474-476.

1173   Raymond, Marcel. "Culture ouverte et langage
       poétique," pp. 9-19 in *Travaux de linguistique et
       de littérature* publiés par le Centre de philologie
       et de littérature romanes de l'Université de
       Strasbourg. 1964. Paris: Klincksieck, 1964.

1174   Rioux, Bertrand. "Ontologie du signifier." *Man
       and World*, vol. IV, Aug. 1971, pp. 243-258.

       Roche, Maurice. *Phenomenology, Language, and the
       Social Sciences*. See 1293a.

1175   Schuetz, Alfred. "Language, language disturbances
       and the texture of consciousness. A philosophi-
       cal interpretation of language disturbances."
       Social Research, vol. XVII, 1950, pp. 380-382.

1176   Stewart, David. "Language and et langage." *Phi-
       losophy Today*, vol. XVIII, Summer 1974, pp. 87-
       105.

       Toscano, Giuseppe. See Italian Books (No. 232).

       Turner, Ingrid Jacqueline. See Dissertation (No.
       336).

1177   Uscatescu, Jorge. "Nuevos aspectos de la fenom-
       enología del lenguaje." *Arbor*, no. 263, Nov.
       1967, pp. 199-211.

1178   Verstraelen, Eugene. "Language analysis and Merleau-
       Ponty's phenomenology of language." *St. Louis
       Quarterly*, vol. IV, 1966, pp. 325-342.

       Viano, Carlo A. See AESTHETICS (No. 906).

LANGUAGE

1179 Waelhens, Alphonse de. "De taalphilosophie volgens M. Merleau-Ponty." *Tijdschrift voor Filosofie*, vol. XVI, no. 4, Supplement 1954, pp. 402-408.

1180 Waelhens, Alphonse de. "La philosophie du langage selon M. Merleau-Ponty," pp. 123-141 in *Existence et signification*. Louvain: E. Nauwelaerts, 1958.

Wahl, François. See STRUCTURALISM (No. 1361).

1181 Welch, Cyril. "Commentary on 'Ontologie du signifier' (B. Rioux)." *Man and World*, vol. IV, Aug. 1971, pp. 258-261.

1182 Wild, John. "Is there a world of ordinary language?" *Philosophical Review*, vol. LVII, no. 4, 1958.

LATER THOUGHT of M-P

1183 Bannan, John F. "The 'later' thought of Merleau-Ponty." *Dialogue*, vol. V, no. 3, Dec. 1966, pp. 383-403.

1184 Martino, Eutimio. "Il pessismismo relativo del último Merleau-Ponty. Apunges de su curso 1958-1959 en el Collège de France." *Pensamiento*, vol. XXVI, no. 101, Jan.-March 1970, pp. 73-88.

1185 Métraux, Alexandre. "Vision and being in the last lectures of Merleau-Ponty," pp. 323-336 in *Life-World and Consciousness. Essays for Aron Gurwitsch*. Edited by Lester E. Embree. Evanston, Ill.: Northwestern University Press, 1972.

1186 Richir, Marc. "Phénoménalisation, distorsion, logologie. Essai sur la dernière pensée de Merleau-Ponty." *Textures* (Braine l'Alleud), vol. IV, no. 4, 1972, pp. 63-114.

Taminiaux, Jacques. See PHENOMENOLOGY (No. 1300).

LEARNING

Meyer, Miles W. See SKINNER (No. 871).

'LECTURES' de M-P

Cotten, Jean-Pierre. See *Phénoménologie* (No. 374).

'LEBENSWELT'

1186 Brand, G. *Die Lebenswelt. Eine Philosophie des konkretes Apriori*. Chapter V. Berlin: Walter de Gruyter, 1970.

Caillois, Roland. See HISTOIRE (No. 1098)

LEFT (the French Left)

1187 Anonymous. "Un homme de la 'nouvelle gauche'." *Le Monde*, 5 mai 1961, p. 1.

1188 Montaldi, Danilo. "Cronache della 'gauche'." *Questioni*, no. 3, May 1956, pp. 4-11.

Sérant, P. "Maurice Merleau-Ponty et la pensée de gauche." See AVENTURES (no. 500).

1189 Steffen, Günther. "Die französische Linke: Mythos und Realität." *Merkur*, no. 99, May 1956, pp. 471-481.

1190 Winner, Percy. "The 'New Left' in France: Why the intellectuals are cooling toward Communism." *The New Republic*, vol. 133, no. 3, July 18, 1955, pp. 14-15.

LITERATURE

1191 Anonymous. "Lettres-arts-spectacles." *Le Nouvel Observateur*, n.s. no. 4, 10 décembre 1964, pp. 30-31.

1192 Anonymous. "Repères." *Le Monde* [*des Livres*], no. 7857, 18 avril 1970, p. 5.

1193 Barrett, William. "The end of modern literature." *Partisan Review*, vol. XVI, Sept. 1949, pp. 942-950.

Boon, James A. See LEVI-STRAUSS (No. 804).

1194 Calhoun, Richard James. "Existentialism, phenomenology and literary theory." *South Atlantic Bulletin*, vol. XXVIII, no. 4, Nov. 1963, pp. 4-8.

1195 Cruikshank, John. "Philosophie et littérature," pp. 5-12, in *Philosophie et littérature*. Deuxième colloque de la Société Britannique de Philosophie de langue française. Hull: Fretwells Ltd., 1963.

1196 Dupriez, B. *L'Etude des styles ou la commutation en littérature*. Paris-Montréal-Bruxelles: Didier, 1969. 333p.

1197 Fanizza, Franco. *Letteratura come filosofia*. Firenze: La Nuova Italia Editrice, 1964. 144p.

LITERATURE

1198   Faye, Jean-Pierre. "Interphones et entrelacs." *Tel Quel*, no. 20, hiver 1965, pp. 84-90.

Iser, Wolfgang. See COMMUNICATION (No. 980).

1199   Knight, Everett W. *Literature considered as Philosophy*. London: Routledge & Kegan Paul, 1957. [on *Phenomenology of Perception*]

1200   Magliola, Robert. "The phenomenological approach to literature: Its theory and methodology." *Language and Style*, vol. V, no. 2, Spring 1972, pp. 79-99.

1201   Major, Jean-Louis. "Le philosophe comme critique littéraire." *Dialogue*, vol. IV, no. 2, Sept. 1965, pp. 230-242.

1202   Micha, René. "Les pouvoirs effectifs de la prose." *L'Arc*, no. 46, 1971, pp. 88-93.

1203   Nichols, Stephen G. "Remembrance of things recreated: Aspects of French New Criticism." *Contemporary Literature*, vol. XI, no. 2, Spring 1970, pp. 243-268.

1204   Oxenhandler, Neal. "The place of literature in the work of Maurice Merleau-Ponty." *Kentucky Romance Quarterly*, vol. XVII, no. 2, 1970, pp. 171-187. Reprinted "Literature as perception in the work of Merleau-Ponty," pp. 229-254 in *Modern French Criticism, from Proust and Valéry to Structuralism*, ed. by John K. Simon. Chicago-London: University of Chicago Press, 1972.

Pingaud, Bernard. "Merleau-Ponty, Sartre et la littérature." See SARTRE (No. 857).

1205   Theobald, David W. "Philosophy and fiction: The novel as eloquent philosophy." *British Journal of Aesthetics*, vol. XIV, Winter 1974, pp. 17-25.

1206   Tilliette, Xavier. *Existence et littérature*. Paris: Desclée de Brouwer, 1962. 205p.

Stubberud, Tore. See Books (No. 257).

<u>LOGOS</u>

Bruzina, Ronald C. See Dissertation (No. 267).

Farrell Krell, David. See EROS (No. 1007).

LOVE

Lapointe, François H. See DESIRE (No. 994).

MAN (see also Anthropology)

1207 Arcaya, Jose. "Two languages of man." *Journal of Phenomenological Psychology*, vol. IV, no. 1, Fall 1973, pp. 315-340.

Aufranc, D. M. See ETHICS (No. 1008).

Epstein, Michèle F. See WITTGENSTEIN (No. 881).

1208 Fernandez, Valeriano Bozal. "M. Merleau-Ponty: la fenomenología y la ciencia del hombre." *Cuadernos Hispanoamericanos*, no. 197, May 1966, pp. 437-442.

1209 Kwant, Remy C. "De mens als oorsprong." *Tijdschrift voor Filosofie*, vol. XXXI, Summer 1969, pp. 441-470.

1210 Maione, Pasquale. "La dimensione archeologica dell'uomo." *Rassegna Scienze Filosofiche*, vol. I, no. 22, 1969, pp. 255-266.

Ricoeur, Paul. See No. 715.

1211 Schrag, Calvin O. "Praxis and structure: Conflicting models in the sciences of man." *Journal of the British Society for Phenomenology*, vol. VI, no. 1, Jan. 1975, pp. 23-31.

Touron del Pie, Eliseo. See Books (No. 245).

MARXISM

(See also *Les Aventures de la dialectique* and *Humanisme et Terreur*)

1212 Aron, Raymond. *L'Opium des intellectuels.* Paris: Gallimard, 1955. English trans. by Terence Kilmartin, *The Opium of the Intellectuals.* New York: Norton, 1962.

1213 Aron, Raymond. "The impact of Marxism in the twentieth century," pp. 1-46 in Milorad M. Drachkovitch, *Marxism in the Modern World.* Stanford, Cal.: Stanford University Press, for Hoover Institution on War, Revolution, and Peace, 1965. Reprinted in *Marxism and the Existentialists,* pp. 111-163.

MARXISM

1214   Aron, Raymond. *Marxismes imaginaires. D'une sainte famille à l'autre.* Paris: Gallimard, 1970.

1215   Aron, Raymond. "Of passions and polemics." *Encounter*, vol. XXXIV, no. 5,

1216   Aron, Raymond. "Marxisme et existentialisme." Lecture given at the Collège Philosophique, 1946. Reprinted in a collective volume entitled, *L'Homme, le monde, et l'histoire.* Paris: Arthuad, 1948. Reprinted pp. 27-61 in *Marxismes imaginaires*, cf supra. English trans. in *Marxism and the Existentialists*, pp. 19-41.

       Aron, Raymond. See LES AVENTURES (No. 469).

       Bien, Joseph. "Le marxisme et la question de la terreur chez Merleau-Ponty." See Dissertation (No. 266).

1217   Botto, Evardo. "*Marxismi immaginari: Da una sacra famiglia all'altra.*" (Review of Aron, cf. supra). *Rivista di Filosofia Neo-Scolastica*, vol. LXIV, Oct.-Dec. 1972, pp. 744-747.

1218   Carruba, Gerald J. "The phenomenological foundations of Marxism in the early works of Maurice Merleau-Ponty." *Dianoia* (Mexico), vol. X, Spring 1974, pp. 37-55.

       Cooper, Fraser B. "Existential phenomenology and Marxism: The politics of Merleau-Ponty." See Dissertation (No. 273).

       Dunne, R. See Dissertation (No. 279).

1219   Duvignaud, Jean. "Der marxistisch-existentialistische Disput," pp. 39-46 in *Französische Kultur 1962.* Köln: Verlag der Dokumente, 1962.

1220   Faracovi, Ornella Pompeo. *Il Marxismo francese contemporaneo fra dialettica e struttura (1945-1968).* Milano: Feltrinelli, 1970.

1221   Faracovi, Ornella Pompeo. "Eresia e riformismo in Merleau-Ponty." *Il Ponte*, anno XXIX, no. 9, Sept. 1973, pp. 1235-1259.

1222   Fergnani, Franco. "Marxismo e 'filosofia dell'ambiguità'." *Il Pensiero Critico*, no. 4, Oct.-Dec. 1960, pp. 16-65.

       Holz, Hans Heinz. See No. 666.

MARXISM   145

1223   Hook, Sidney. "Marxism in the western world: From
       'scientific socialism' to mythology," pp. 1-36, in
       Milorad M. Drachkovitch, ed., *Marxist Ideology in
       the Contemporary World--Its Appeals and Paradoxes.*
       New York: Frederick A. Praeger Pub., 1966.

1124   Iglesias, Juan Andrès. "Le marxisme acommuniste de
       Merleau-Ponty." *Akten XIV.* International Kongress
       Philosophie, 2-9 Sept. 1968. pp. 62-68 in *Proceedings of the 14th International Congress for
       Philosophy.* Vienna: Herder, 1968. xv-688p.

       Kuhn, H. See EXISTENTIALISM (No. 1068).

       Olafson, Frederick A. See HISTORY (No. 1101).

       Papi, Fulvio. See FREEDOM (No. 1083).

1225   Pieri, Sergio. "*Il Marxismo francese contemporaneo,*
       Ornella Pompeo Faracovi." *Giornale Critico della
       Filosofia Italiana,* vol. LII, Jan.-March 1973,
       pp. 145-149.

1226   Puente, Ojea G. "Fenomenología y marxismo en el
       pensamiento de Merleau-Ponty." *Cuadernos Hispanoamericanos*, no. 26, 1956, pp. 295-326, and *Ibid.*,
       no. 29, 1956, pp. 221-256.

       Puente, Ojea G. See EXISTENTIALISM (No. 1051).

       Robbins, Jack A. "Merleau-Ponty on Marxism 1945-
       1955." See Dissertation (No. 326).

1227   Scarpelli, U. *Esistenzialismo e marxismo. Saggio
       sulla giustizia.* Torino: Taylor, 1968, 3a ed.
       1970.

       Semerari, Giuseppe. See PHEN (Nos. 408 and 409).

1228   Suppo, A. Review of Scarpelli cf supra. *Filosofia*
       (Torino), vol. XX, 1969, pp. 639-642.

       Surkim, Marvin L. See Dissertation (No. 332).

       Traub, Essen O. See Dissertation (No. 335).

       Valentini, Francesco. See EXISTENTIALISM (No. 1058).

       Waelhens, Alphonse de. See EXISTENTIALISM (No. 1061).

       Young, Marlene. See Dissertation (No. 338).

MASCULINE & FEMININE

1229 Walsh, Margaret Ann. See Dissertation (No. 337).

MATERIALISM

Bien, Joseph. See ECONOMIC (No. 1005).

1230 Bonomi, Andrea. "Materialismo storico e questione esistenziale." *Aut Aut*, no. 75, 1963, pp. 66-73.

MEANING

Derossi, Giorgio. See 1250.

Panaccio, Claude. See STRUCTURE (No. 1363).

METAPHOR

Edie, James M. See EXPRESSION (No. 1073).

Romanyshyn, Robert D. See BEHAVIOR (No. 939).

METAPHYSICS

Good, Paul. See Dissertation (No. 290).

Kwant, Remy C. See Books (No. 142).

METHOD

Fairchild, David L. See Dissertation, Austin (No. 282).

Murphy, Richard T. See Dissertation (No. 317).

Sapontzis, Steve F. See Dissertation (No. 328).

1231 Vuillemin, Jules. "La méthode indirecte de Merleau-Ponty." *Critique*, no. 211, decembre 1964, pp. 1007-1016.

MIND

Johanning, J. C. See Dissertation (No. 298).

MONISM

Bertram, Maryane J. See Dissertation (No. 264).

MUSIC

Lefeuvre, M. See LEVI-STRAUSS (No. 806).

NOVEL

1231 Pollman, Leo. *Der französische Roman im 20. Jahrhundert. Entwurf einer Geschichte des mythischen Selbstverständnisses unserer Zeit.* Stuttgart, Köln, Mainz: Verlag W. Kohlhammer, 1970. 216p.

Theobald, David W. See LITERATURE.

OBJECT

1232 Dumas, J.-L. "Les conférences." *La Nef*, vol. V, no. 45, aout 1949, pp. 150-151. [A summary by Dumas of a lecture given by Merleau-Ponty entitled 'L'homme et l'objet."]

1233 Smith, Colin. "La notion d'objet chez Merleau-Ponty," pp. 27-31 in *Premier Colloque* de la Société Britannique de Philosophie de langue française. *Actes. Résumés* des communications. Hull: Fretwells, Ltd., 1962.

1234 Smith, Colin. "The notion of object in the phenomenology of Merleau-Ponty." *Philosophy*, vol. 39, no. 148, April 1964, pp. 110-119.

1235 Wells, Rulon. "World and object." *Review of Metaphysics*, vol. XIV, no. 4, issue 56, pp. 695-703.

'NOUVEAU ROMAN'

Carrabino, Victor. See Phenomenology (No. 1265).

OBJECTIVISM

Patocka, J. See PSYCHOLOGY (No. 1331).

OBJECTIVITY

Houghton, Giles K. See Dissertation (No. 293).

ONTOLOGY (see also Being)

1236 Cantista, Maria José. "Reflexão sobre a ontologia de Merleau-Ponty." *Revista Portuguesa de Filosofia*, vol. XXVII, July-Sept. 1971, pp. 289-299.

Casalis, Mathieu. See DEVELOPMENT (No. 995).

1237 Derossi, Giorgio. "Dalla percezione alla visione: L'ontologia negativa dell'ultimo Merleau-Ponty." *Filosofia* (Torino), vol. XVI, 1965, pp. 333-357 [*Le Visible et l'Invisible*.]

ONTOLOGY

Dillon, Martin C. See Dissertation (No. 277).

Flynn, Bernard. "The question of ontology," pp. 114-126 in Gillan Books (No. 135).

Friedman, Robert Malcolm. See Dissertations (No. 284).

Gallagher, Donald K. See Dissertations (No. 287).

Gillespie, M. L. See No. 289.

Heidsieck, François. See French Books (No. 181).

1238 Kaelin, Eugene. "Merleau-Ponty, fundamental ontologist." *Man and World*, vol. III, Fall 1970, pp. 102-115.

1239 Lowry, Atherton C. "Merleau-Ponty and fundamental ontology." *International Philosophical Quarterly*, vol. XV, no. 4, Dec. 1975.

Métraux, Alexandre. See LATER THOUGHT (No. 1185).

Penati, Giancarlo. See Lavelle Italian Books (No. 229).

Pilz, Georg M. See German Books (No. 207).

Rada Donath, Alejandro. See Dissertations (No. 324).

Rioux, Bertrand. See LANGUAGE (No. 1174).

Sheridan, James F. See SARTRE (No. 501).

Welch, Cyril. See LANGUAGE (No. 1181).

ORIGINS (the problem of)

1240 Busch, T. W. "Merleau-Ponty and the problem of origins." *Philosophy Today*, vol. XI, no. 2, Summer 1967, pp. 124-130.

Kwant, Remy C. See MAN (No. 1209).

THE OTHER (see also Intersubjectivity)

1241 Bakker, Reinout. "De leer van 'de ander' in de fenomenologie van Merleau-Ponty," pp. 86-88, in *Handelengen v. h. 25e Nederlands Filologencongres*, 1958. Groningen: Wolters, 1958.

1242   Bakker, Reinout. "Der andere Mensch in der Phanomenologie Merleau-Pontys." *Evangelische Ethik*, Heft 1, 1960, pp. 10-26.

1243   Caruso, Paolo. "Il problema dell'esistenza altrui in Merleau-Ponty." *Aut Aut*, no. 66, Nov. 1961, pp. 567-576.

1244   Ferraris, Anna. "L'apertura all'alterità nella filosofia di Merleau-Ponty," pp. 249-291, in *Atti dell'Academia delle Scienze di Torino*, Classe di Sc. Mor., stor., e filos., vol. 97, 1962-1963, pp. 249-291.

1245   Finance, Joseph de. *L'Affrontement de l"autre. Essai sur l'altérité*. Rome: Universita Gregoriana Editrice, 1973.

Fileasi, Paolo. See *Les relations de l'enfant avec autrui* (No. 603).

Johanning, J. C. See Dissertations (No. 298).

1246   Laín Entralgo, Pedro. "Maurice Merleau-Ponty," in *Teoria y realidad del otro*, I, 2a p., chapter 4. Madrid: Revista de Occidente, 1961.

1247   Lapointe, François. "The Existence of alter egos: Jean-Paul Sartre and Maurice Merleau-Ponty." *Journal of Phenomenological Psychology*, vol. VI, Spring 1976.

1248   Letayf, S. "Le problème du moi et de l'autre." *Revista da Universidade Catolica de Sao Paolo*, vol. VI, 1954, pp. 87-93.

PAINTING (see Aesthetics also)

Kaufman, Pierre. See L'Oeil (No. 539).

Klein, Robert. See L'Oeil (No. 540).

Kwant, Remy C. De stemmen der stilte. See Books Dutch (Nos. 253 and 254).

Lefeuvre, M. See LEVI-STRAUSS (No. 806).

Place, James Gordon. See Dissertations (No. 321).

1249   Place, James Gordon. "Merleau-Ponty and the spirit of painting." *Philosophy Today*, vol. XVII, Winter 1973, pp. 280-290.

PAROLE (see Language also)

Cowley, Fraser. See EXPRESSION (No. 1072).

PERCEPTION (see Phénoménologie de la perception)

Brena, Gian L. See Books.

Burgers, Antoon. See BERGSON (No. 765).

1250   Derossi, Giorgio. "L'emergenza del percepito e del significato dal progetto intenzionale corporeo in Merleau-Ponty." *Filosofia* (Torino), vol. XV, 1964, pp. 127-153.

Fressin, A. See Books (No. 217).

1251   Haymond, William S. "Merleau-Ponty on sensory perception." *The Modern Schoolman*, vol. 44, no. 2, Jan. 1967, pp. 93-111.

Houghton, Giles K. See OBJECTIVITY (No. 293).

Johanning, J. C. See Dissertations (No. 298).

1252   Kockelmans, Joseph. "Merleau-Ponty's view on space perception and space." *Review of Existential Psychology and Psychiatry*, vol. IV, no. 1, Feb. 1964, pp. 69-105.

1253   Kockelmans, Joseph. "Merleau-Ponty and space perception," pp. 274-311 in *Phenomenology and the natural sciences. Essays and translations.* Edited by J. Kockelmans and Theodore Kisiel. Evanston, Ill.: Northwestern University Press, 1970.

1254   Kockelmans, Joseph. "Ruimtewaarneming en ruimte volgens Merleau-Ponty." *Tijdschrift voor Filosofie*, vol. XIX, no. 3, 1957, pp. 372-427.

1255   Lattre, Alain de. "L'univers de la perception et ses dimensions chez Merleau-Ponty." *Revue Philosophique de la France et de l'Etranger*, CLXIV, 1974, pp. 273-294.

1256   McCurdy, John D. "Synergetic perception." *Journal of Phenomenological Psychology*, vol. III, no. 2, Spring 1973, pp. 217-246.

1257   Schimong, Abner. "Perception from an evolutionary point of view." *Journal of Philosophy*, vol. LXVIII, Oct. 1971, pp. 571-583.

1258   Sinding, Stephan. "Sur notre savoir perceptif."
        Revue de Métaphysique et de Morale, vol. 76,
        Jan.-March 1971, pp. 99-112.

1259   Ver Eecke, Wilfried. "Interpretation and perception." *International Philosophical Quarterly*,
        vol. XI, no. 3, Sept. 1971, pp. 372-384.

        Reboul, Olivier. See ALAIN (No. 756).

        Yoltin, John. See 755a.

        PESSIMISM

        Martino, Eutimio. See LATER Thought (No. 1184).

        PHENOMENOLOGY

1260   Alexander, Ian W. "The phenomenological philosophy
        in France. An analysis of its themes, significance and implications," pp. 325-352 in T. V.
        Benn, ed., *Currents of Thought in French Literature.* Essays in Memory of G. T. Clapton. Oxford:
        Basil Blackwell- New York: Barnes & Noble, 1965.

1261   Bannan, John F. "Philosophical reflection and the
        phenomenology of Merleau-Ponty." *Review of Metaphysics*, vol. VIII, no. 3, March 1955, pp. 411-442.

1262   Bannan, John F. "Merleau-Ponty mismanaged." *Journal
        of Existentialism*, vol. VII, Summer 1967, pp.
        459-472 [cf. R. Schmit]

1263   Berger, Gaston. "L'originalité de la phénoménologie."
        Les Etudes Philosophiques, vol. IX, 1954, pp.
        249-259.

        Bertoldi, Eugene. "Merleau-Ponty and the phenomenology of phenomenology." See Dissertation (No.
        263).

        Bornheim, Gerd A. See CAUSALITY (No. 969).

1264   Bucio, Palomino F. "Postura fenomenologica de M.
        Merleau-Ponty." *Humanitas*, vol. VIII, 1967, pp.
        35-45.

        Calhoun, Richard J. See LITERATURE (No. 1194).

1265   Carrabino, Victor. "Phenomenology and the 'Nouveau
        Roman': A moment of epiphany." *South Atlantic
        Bulletin*, Vol. XXXVII, no. 4, Nov. 1973, pp. 95-100.

1265a   Carter, John E. "Philosophical and psychological theories of phenomenology." *Proceedings of Philosophy of Education*, vol. XXX, 1974, pp. 137-147.

Corriveau, Michael. See SKINNER (No. 869).

1266   Crosson, Frederick J. "Phenomenology and realism." *International Philosophical Quarterly*, vol. VI, Sept. 1966, pp. 455-464.

1267   Cuervo Jean, Elina. "Fenomenología y psicoanalisis." *Philosophia*, Revista del Instituto de Filosofía de la Universidad Nacional de Cuyo, Mendoza, no. 35, 1969, pp. 162-169.

1268   Culler, Jonathan. "Phenomenology and structuralism." *Human Context, Le Domaine Humain*, vol. V, Spring 1973, pp. 35-41.

1269   Daly, James. "Merleau-Ponty's concept of phenomenology." *Philosophical Studies* (Maynooth), vol. XVI, 1967, pp. 137-164.

1270   Daly, James. "Merleau-Ponty: A bridge between phenomenology and structuralism." *Journal of the British Society for Phenomenology*, vol. II, no. 3, Oct. 1971, pp. 53-58.

Earle, William. See EXISTENTIALISM (No. 1037).

1271   Edie, James M. "Recent developments in phenomenology." *American Philosophical Quarterly*, vol. I, no. 2, April 1964, pp. 115-128.

1272   Farber, Marvin. *The Foundation of Phenomenology*. New York: Paine Whitman Pub., 1962.

1273   Farber, Marvin. *Phenomenology and Existence. Toward a Philosophy Within Nature*. New York: Harper & Row, Harper Torchbooks, 1967.

Fernandez, Valeriano Bozal. See MAN (No. 1208).

1274   Funari, E. A. "Fenomenologia e psicologia della visione." *Aut Aut*, no. 74, 1963, pp. 95-104.

1275   Granel, G. "Le psychologique et le phénoménologique." *Annales de la Faculté des Lettres de Toulouse*, tome IV, 1965, pp. 101-113.

1276   Gurwitsch, Aron. *The Field of Consciousness*. Pittsburgh: Duquesne University Press, 1964.

1277   Gurwitsch, Aron. *Studies in Phenomenology and Psychology*. Evanston, Ill.: Northwestern University Press, 1966.

1278   Hayen, André. "La phénoménologie de Merleau-Ponty et la métaphysique." *Revue Philosophique de Louvain*, vol. L, no. 25, Feb. 1952, pp. 102-123.

1279   Jeanson, Francis. *La Phénoménologie*. Paris: Téqui, 1951.

Kwant, Remy C. See English and Dutch Books (Nos. 142, 143, 252, and 255).

1280   Kwant, Remy C. "Merleau-Ponty and phenomenology," pp. 375-392 in *Phenomenology*, ed. by Joseph J. Kockelmans. Garden City: Doubleday, Anchor Books, 1967. Reprinted from Kwant's *The Phenomenological Philosophy of Merleau-Ponty*, pp. 153-168.

Langan, Thomas. See EXISTENTIALISM (No. 1044).

1281   Lauer, Quentin. "Four phenomenologists." *Thought*, vol. XXXIII, Summer 1958, pp. 183-204.

1282   Lomba Fuentes, Joaquín. "Fenomenología existencial en Merleau-Ponty." *Pensamiento* (Madrid), vol. XXVII, July-Sept. 1971, pp. 309-331.

1283   Luipjen, W. *Existentiele phaenomenologie*. Utrecht, 1959. English trans. by Henry Koren, *Existential Phenomenology*. Pittsburgh: Duquesne University Press, 1960.

Luipjen, W. See ATHEISM (No. 933).

1284   Luipjen, W. *Phenomenology and Metaphysics*, pp. 38-54, 156-163. Pittsburgh: Duquesne University Press, 1965.

1285   Lyotard, Jean-François. "Phénoménologie et psychologie," chapter 2 in *La Phénoménologie*. Paris: Presses Universitaires de France, 1954.

Madison, Gary B. See French Books (No. 186).

Magliola, Robert. See LITERATURE (No. 1200).

Mansion, Suzanne. See ARISTOTLE (No. 759).

Marini, A. See HUSSERL (No. 789).

1286   Mizuno, K. "What is the phenomenology of Merleau-
        Ponty?" *Memoirs Osaka Galugei University*, Cult.
        Soc. Sci., vol. XIV, 1965, pp. 78-102 [In Japan-
        ese, Summary in French.]

1286a   Monasterio, X. O. "Paradoxes et mythes de la phé-
        noménologie." *Revue de Métaphysique et de Morale*,
        vol. 72, no. 4, juillet-septembre 1969, pp. 268-
        280.

1287   Montull, Tomas. "Merleau-Ponty: Fenomenología y
        campo fenoménico." *Estudios Filosóficos*, vol.
        XIII, 1964, pp. 41-80.

1288   Moreau, Joseph. "Phénoménologie et idéalisme."
        Giornale di Metafisica, vol. XV, no. 5, 1960,
        pp. 557-575.

        Morriston, Charles Wesley. "Phenomenology and the
        problem of the external world." See Dissertations
        (No. 315).

        Murphy, Richard T. See Dissertations (No. 317).

        Negri, A. See KANT (No. 800).

1289   O'Neill, John. "Can phenomenology be critical?"
        Philosophy of Social Sciences, vol. II, March
        1972, pp. 1-13.

1289a   Palermo, James. "Direct experience in the open class-
        room. A phenomenological description." *Proceed-
        ings of Philosophy of Education*, vol. XXX, 1974,
        pp. 241-254.

        Passmore, John. See EXISTENTIALISM (No. 1050).

        Philippe, M. D. See PHEN de la P (Nos. 399 and 400).

1290   Piana, G. *I problemi della fenomenologia*. Milan:
        Mondadori, 1967.

        Piorkowski, Henry. See HUSSERL (No. 792).

        Puente, Ojea G. See MARXISM (No. 1226).

        Rada Donath, Alejandro. See Dissertations (No. 324).

1291   Ricoeur, Paul. "Sur la phénoménologie." *Esprit*, vol.
        XXI, no. 12, decembre 1953, pp. 821-829.

1292   Ricoeur, Paul. "Phénoménologie existentielle," pp.
        3-12 in *Encyclôpedie Française: Philosophie-
        Religion*, vol. 19. Paris: Librairie Larousse,
        1957.

1293   Robert, Jean Dominique. "Sciences humaines et phénoménologie." *Revue Philosophique de Louvain*, vol. LXVI, 1968, pp. 102-123.

1293a Roche, Maurice. *Phenomenology, Language, and the Social Sciences*. London: Routledge & Kegan Paul, 1973 (pp. 25-28, 127-134, 162-170, 265-270 and passim).

Roth, John K. See FARBER (No. 772).

Sallis, John. See Books (No. 161).

Sandrini, F. See Dissertations (No. 327).

Schilardi de Barcena, Maria. "Merleau-Ponty: La fenomenología en su ultima obra." See LE Visible (No. 574).

1294   Schmitt, Richard. "Maurice Merleau-Ponty." (two parts). *Review of Metaphysics*, vol. XIX, no. 3, March 1966, pp. 491-516; and *Ibid.*, vol. XIX, no. 4, June 1966, pp. 728-741. [See Bannan's response.]

1295   Schmitt, Richard. "Phenomenology," pp. 135-151, in *The Encyclopedia of Philosophy*. Ed. Paul Edwards, New York: The Macmillan Co. and The Free Press, 1967, vol. 6.

1296   Semerari, Giuseppe. "Critica e projetto dell'uomo nella fenomenologia di Maurice Merleau-Ponty." *Il Pensiero*, vol. V, no. 3, Sept.-Dec. 1960, pp. 329-359.

1297   Sinari, Ramakant. "The phenomenology of Merleau-Ponty." *Philosophic Quarterly* (India), vol. 39 no. 2, July 1966, pp. 129-140.

Spiegelberg, Herbert. See HUSSERL (no. 794).

1298   Spiegelberg, Herbert. "The phenomenological philosophy of Maurice Merleau-Ponty," pp. 516-560, vol. 2, in *The Phenomenological Movement. A Historical Introduction*. The Hague: Martinus Nijhoff, 1960.

1299   Strasser, Stephen. *Phenomenology and the Human Sciences*. English trans. by Henry Koren. Pittsburgh: Duquesne University Press, 1963.

Struyker Boudier, C. E. M. See Dutch Books (No. 256).

PHENOMENOLOGY

1300   Taminiaux, Jacques. "Phenomenology in Merleau-Ponty's late work," pp. 307-322 in *Life-World and Consciousness*. Essays for Aron Gurwitsch. Edited by Lester E. Embree. (Northwestern University Studies in Phenomenology and Existential Philosophy). Evanston, Ill.: Northwestern University Press, 1972.

1301   Thévenaz, Pierre. "Qu'est-ce que la phénoménologie?" *Revue de Théologie et de Philosophie*, 3e série, 1952, pp. 294-316.

1302   Thévenaz, Pierre. "Maurice Merleau-Ponty," in *De Husserl à Merleau-Ponty. Qu'est-ce que la phénoménologie?* Introd. de Jean Brun. Neuchâtel: Les Editions de la Baconnière, 1966. English trans. *What is Phenomenology? and Other Essays*. Edited with an introduction [and notes] by James M. Edie. Preface by John Wild. Chicago: Quadrangle Books, 1963, 191p.

1303   Tillman, F. "Phenomenology and philosophical analysis." *International Philosophical Quarterly*, vol. VI, 1966, pp. 465-482.

1304   Tymieniecka, Ann-T. *Phenomenology and Sciences in Contemporary European Thought*. New York: Noonday Press, 1962.

Urango, E. See EXISTENTIALISM (No. 1057).

Vircilio, Domenico. See HUSSERL (No. 798).

Waelhens, Alphonse de. See EXISTENTIALISME (No. 1060).

Wild, John. See EXISTENCE (No. 1021).

Yagüe, Joaquín. See Book, Spanish (No. 247).

PHILOSOPHY

Bakker, Reinout. See Noodzakelijke, 1965, Dutch Books (No. 250, 251).

Dallery, Robert Carleton. See Dissertations (No. 275).

1305   Kisiel, Theodore. "Merleau-Ponty on philosophy and science," pp. 251-273 in *Phenomenology and the Natural Sciences*. Essays and translations. Edited by Joseph Kockelmans and Theodore Kisiel. Evanston, Ill.: Northwestern University Press, 1970.

1306   Kwant, Remy C. "De autonomie van de wijsbegeerte volgens Merleau-Ponty." *Algemeen Nederlands Tijdschrift voor Wijsbegeerte en Psychologie*, vol. LVIII, 1966, pp. 122-135. Also in *Annalen van het Genootschap voor Wetenschappelijke Philosophie*, vol. XXXVI, 1966, pp. 122-135.

1307   Kwant, Remy C. "De verhouding tussen wijsbegeerte en psychologie in het denken van Maurice Merleau-Ponty." *Annalen van het Thijmgenootschapp*, vol. 45, no. 2, 1957, pp. 164-181.

1308   Muglioni, J. "Merleau-Ponty fût-il philosophe?" *Revue Socialiste*, no. 146, octobre 1961, pp. 272-275.

1309   Murguia, Adolfo. "Acerca de la muerte de la filosofía." *Revista de Occidente*, vol. XXXIX, no. 116, Nov. 1972, pp. 234-243.

Pietersma, Henry. See HUSSERL (No. 791).

1310   Robert, Jean Dominique. "Le sort de la philosophie à l'heure des sciences de l'homme." *Revue des Sciences Philosophiques et Théologiques*, vol. 41, octobre 1967, pp. 573-616.

Semerari, Giuseppe. See PHEN (No. 410).

Spiegelberg, Herbert. See EXISTENTIALISM (No. 1054).

1310a   Strasser, Stephen. "Merleau-Ponty's bijdrage tot de sociaalfilosofie. Interpretatie en critiek." *Tijdschrift voor Filosofie*, vol. XXIX, 1967, pp. 427-470.

POLITICS (also Marxism, French Left, Social Thought)

1311   Burnier, Michel-Antoine. *Les existentialistes et la politique*. Paris: Gallimard, 1966. English trans. by Bernard Murchland, *Choice of Action. The French Existentialists on the Political Front Line*. Additional chapter by Bernard Murchland, "Sartre and Camus: The anatomy of a quarrel." New York: Random House, 1968.

Cooper, Fraser B. See Dissertations (No. 273).

Faracovi, See MARXISM (No. 1221).

Goyard, Pierre. See DEVELOPMENT (No. 997).

1312   Hervé, Pierre. "Sommes-nous tous des coquins?" *L'Action, Hebdomadaire de l'Indépendance française*, 15 février 1946, pp. 1-2.

POLITICS

Howard, Dick. "Ambiguous radicalism: Merleau-Ponty's interrogation of political thought," pp. 143-159 in Gillan Book (No. 135).

Howard, Dick. See LEFORT (No. 803).

Invitto, Giovanni. See Italian Books (No. 226).

1313 Jung, Hwa Yol. "The radical humanization of politics: Merleau-Ponty's philosophy of politics." *Archiv für Rechts-und Sozialphilosophie*, vol. LIII, no. 2, 1967, pp. 233-256.

1314 Lefort, Claude. "La politique et la pensée de la politique." *Les Lettres Nouvelles*, XIe année, n.s. no. 32, septembre-octobre 1964, pp. 32-34.

1315 Mauriac, François. *Le nouveau bloc-notes, 1961-1964*. Paris: Flammarion, 1968.

1316 McLean, E. B. "Hwa Yol Jung, ed., *Existential phenomenology and Political Theory*." *Political Theory*, vol. I, May 1973, pp. 222-225.

1317 O'Donnell, Donat. "France as the conscience of Europe." *The Listener*, vol. LIII, no. 1351, Jan. 20, 1958, pp. 105-106.

Pauls, Arleen Laura. See Dissertations (No. 319).

Pompei, Paolo. See ETHICS (No. 1016).

Robbins, Jack A. See Dissertations (No. 326).

Sheridan, James F. See Les Aventures (No. 501).

Surkim, Marvin L. See Dissertations (No. 332).

Traub, Essen O. See Dissertations (No. 335).

Wahl, Jean. See EXISTENTIALISME (No. 1063).

Young, Marlene. See Dissertations (No. 338).

PORNOGRAPHY

1318 Hamrick, William S. "Fascination, fear and pornography: A phenomenological typology." *Man and World*, vol. VII, Fall 1974, pp. 52-66.

PORTRAIT

1319 Laporte, Roger. "Merleau-Ponty," in *Quinze variations sur un thème biographique*. (Collection "Textes"). Paris: Flammarion, 1975.

PRAXIS

Ollero Tassara, Andrès. See Spanish Book (No. 241).

Schrag, Calvin O. See MAN (No. 1211).

Walter, Emil H. See HABERMAS (No. 775).

PRE-OBJECTIVE

Ballard, Edward G. See COGNITION (No. 972).

1319 Kullman, Michael, and Taylor, Charles. "The pre-objective world." *Review of Metaphysics*, vol. XII, no. 1, Sept. 1958, pp. 108-132. Reprinted in Maurice Natanson, ed., *Essays in Phenomenology*, pp. 116-136. The Hague: Martinus Nijhoff, 1966.

1320 Kullman, Michael, and Taylor, Charles. "Reply to T. N. Munson." *Review of Metaphysics*, vol. XII, June 1959, pp. 624-632.

1321 Munson, Thomas N. "The pre-objective reconsidered." *Review of Metaphysics*, vol. XII, no. 4, June 1959, pp. 624-632.

Sallis, John. See Books (No. 161).

PRE-REFLEXIVE

Murphy, Richard T. See Dissertations (No. 317).

Sallis, John. See Books (No. 161).

PSYCHIC

1322 Grégoire, François. "Le point de vue phénoménologique," chapter 6 in *La Nature du psychique*. Paris: Presses Universitaires de France, 1957.

PSYCHOANALYSIS

Cuervo Jean, Elina. See PHENOMENOLOGY (No. 1267).

Struyker Boudier, C. E. M. See Dutch Books (No. 256).

PSYCHOLOGY

Arcaya, José. See MAN (No. 1207).

Bouet, Michel M. See INTERIORITY (No. 1141).

POLITICS

1323   Bucklew, J. "The subjective tradition in Phenomenological psychology." *Philosophy of Science*, vol. XXII, 1955, pp. 288-289.

Cantwell, O. F. See Dissertations (No. 270).

Cazabon, Gilles. See BEHAVIOR (No. 937).

Dillon, Martin C. See INTENTIONALITY, GESTALT THEORY (No. 1087).

Fernandez, Valeriano Bozal. See MAN (No. 1208).

Funari, E. A. See PHENOMENOLOGY (No. 1274).

Granel, G. See PHENOMENOLOGY (No. 1275).

Gurwitsch, Aron. PHEN (Nos. 386, 387).

Kwant, Remy C. See PHILOSOPHY (No. 1307).

1324   Lapointe, François H. "Merleau-Ponty's phenomenological critique of psychology." *Journal of Phenomenological Psychology*, vol. II, no. 2, Spring 1972, pp. 237-255.

1325   Lapointe, François H. "The phenomenological psychology of Merleau-Ponty: a bibliography." *'Diálôgos*, vol. VIII, no. 23, 1972, pp. 161-182.

1326   Lapointe, François H. "A selected bibliography on the existential and phenomenological psychology of Maurice Merleau-Ponty." *Journal of Phenomenological Psychology*, vol. III, 1972-1973, pp. 113-130.

1327   Levy, Charles Eric. "Toward primordial reality as the ground of psychological phenomenon." *Journal of Phenomenological Psychology*, vol. III, no. 2, Spring 1973, pp. 173-186. See LE VISIBLE.

Lyotard, Jean-François. See PHENOMENOLOGY (No. 1285).

Marini, A. See HUSSERL (No. 789).

1328   McCurdy, John D. "The sensory media." *Journal of the British Society for Phenomenology*, vol. III, no. 2, May 1972, pp. 165-186.

McCurdy, John D. See PERCEPTION (No. 1256).

Meyer, Miles W. See SKINNER (No. 871).

1329   Mischel, Theodore. "Merleau-Ponty's phenomenological psychology." *Journal of the History of the Behavioral Sciences*, vol. II, 1966, pp. 172-176.

1330   Misiak, Henryk, and Sexton, Virginia Staudt. *Phenomenological, Existential and Humanistic Psychologies. A Historical Survey.* New York: Grune & Stratton, 1973.

Montpellier, Gérard de. See No. 938.

1331   Patocka, J. "Die Kritik des psychologischen Objektivismus und das Problem des phänomenologischen Psychologie bei Sartre und Merleau-Ponty," pp. 175-184 in *Akten XIVth International Congress of Philosophy*, Vienna, Sept. 2-9, 1968. *Proceedings of the 14th International Congress of Philosophy*. Vienna: Herder, 1968.

1332   Piaget, Jean. *Sagesse et illusions de la philosophie.* Paris: Presses Universitaires de France, 1965. English trans. by Wolfe Mays, *Insights and illusions of Philosophy*. New York-Cleveland: The World Publishing Co., 1971.

Rauch, Leo. See Dissertations (No. 325).

1333   Ravagnan, Luis Maria. "La psicología fenomenólogica, Merleau-Ponty," in the appendix to the Spanish Edition of Edna Heidbreder, *Psicologías del Siglo XX*, pp. 487-506. Buenos Aires: Paidós, 1960.

Robert, Jean-Dominique. See No. 1293.

Robert, Jean-Dominique. See No. 1310.

Roche, Maurice. See No. 1293a.

Schrag, Calvin O. See MAN (No. 1211).

Silverman, Hugh J. See Dissertations (No. 330).

Strasser, Stephen. See PHENOMENOLOGY (No. 1299).

1334   Strasser, Stephen. "Phenomenological trends in European Psychology." *Philosophy and Phenomenological Research*, vol. XVIII, no. 1, Sept. 1957, pp. 18-34.

Tibbetts, Paul. See CONSCIOUSNESS (Nos. 989 and 990).

Vircilio, Domenico. See phenomenology HUSSERL (No. 798).

162　POLITICS

　　　　Waelhens, Alphonse de. "Note pour introduire la discussion du rapport de M. Patocka," pp. 225-226, see PATOCKA (No. 1331).

　　　　PSYCHOSOMATICS (see also body, body soul, dualism)

1335　　Carp, EADE. "Remarks on Psychosomatics." *Acta Psychotherapeutica, Psychosomatica, & Orthopaedagogica*, vol. IX, 1961, pp. 66-73.

　　　　REALISM

　　　　Crosson, Frederick J. See PHENOMENOLOGY (No. 1266).

1336　　Kwant, Remy C. "Transcendeert Merleau-Ponty het realisme?" *Tijdschrift voor Filosofie*, vol. XVI, Supplement 1954, pp. 234-263. [Summary in English]

　　　　Minhinnick, J. See Dissertations (No. 314).

　　　　REASON

1337　　Duméry, Henry. *Raison et religion dans la philosophie de l'action*. Paris: Editions du Seuil, 1963. 639p.

　　　　Langan, Thomas. See Books (No. 146).

　　　　Smith, Colin. See EXPRESSION, CONCEPT (No. 983).

　　　　REDUCTION (Husserlian)

　　　　Devetterre, Raymond J. See HUSSERL (No. 783).

　　　　Kwant, Remy C. See HUSSERL (No. 788).

1338　　Waelhens, Alphonse de. "De reductie tot de natuurlijke wereld bij Merleau-Ponty." *Tijdschrift voor Philosophie*, vol. XII, 1950, pp. 447-477.

1339　　Waelhens, Alphonse de. "Zijn verhouding tot Husserl en de fenomenologische reductie." *Tijdschrift voor Filosofie*, vol. XII, 1950, pp. 478-503.

　　　　REFLECTION

　　　　Bannan, John F. See PHENOMENOLOGY (No. 1261)

　　　　Ceriotto, C. L. See LANGUAGE (No. 1148).

　　　　Caillois, See La Phénoménologie de la P (No. 369).

　　　　Herbenick, Raymond. "Merleau-Ponty and the primacy of reflection," pp. 92-113, in Gillan book (No. 135).

RELIGION (see absolute, God, atheism)

Duméry, Henry. See RAISON (No. 1337).

1340 Duméry, Henry. *La foi n'est pas un cri.* Paris: Castermann, 1957.

Zeiler, M. Judith. See Dissertations (No. 339).

SCIENCE

Bakker, Reinout. See No. 250.

Bruzina, Ronald C. pp. 160-174 in Gillan Book (No. 135).

Burgers, Antoon. See BERGSON (No. 765).

1341 Heelan, Patrick A. "Towards a hermeneutic of natural science. *Journal of the British Society for Phenomenology,* vol. III, no. 3, Oct. 1972, pp. 252-260.

Kisiel, Theodore. See PHILOSOPHY (No. 1305).

Pilz, Georg M. See German Books (No. 207).

Semerari, Giuseppe. See PHEN de la P (No. 410).

1342 Struyker Boudier, C. E. M. "Enkele aspeckten van Merleau-Ponty's wetenschapskritiek." *Gawein,* vol. XVIII, 1970, pp. 147-168.

Tymieniecka, A.-T. See PHENOMENOLOGY (No. 1304).

SELF (see The Other)

Hurst, William J. "The self in the philosophy of Merleau-Ponty." See Dissertations (No. 295).

1343 Rice, Philip Blair. "Existentialism and the self." *Kenyon Review,* vol. XII, no. 2, 1950, pp. 304-330.

SEMIOTIC

Carruba, Gerald J. See Dissertation (No. 271).

Lanigan, Richard L. See Dissertation and Book (No. 151).

SENSORY MEDIA

SENSORY MEDIA

1344 McCurdy, John D. "The sensory media." *Journal of the British Society for Phenomenology*, vol. III, no. 2, May 1972, pp. 165-187.

SEXUALITY

1345 Kockelmans, Joseph J. "Merleau-Ponty on sexuality." *Journal of Existentialism,* vol. VI, no. 21, Fall 1965, pp. 9-30.

MacGuigan, M. "The foundations of sexuality. Merleau-Ponty's conception of sexuality and its place in his philosophy." Ph.D. Dissertation, University of Ottawa, 1975. See Dissertations (No. 306).

Walsh, Margaret Ann. "Foundation sexuality: The chiasm of masculine and feminine." See Dissertation (No. 337).

SHAME

1346 Drevet, Claude. "La honte." *Revue de Métaphysique et de Morale*, vol. 74, octobre-décembre 1969, pp. 406-416.

SIGNIFICANCE (of Merleau-Ponty)

1347 Antuñes, M. "Signifição de Maurice Merleau-Ponty." *Brotéria*, vol. 74, no. 5, 1962, pp. 546-560.

SOCIAL THOUGHT

1348 Hughes, Stuart H. *The Obstructed Path: French Social Thought in the Years of Desperation, 1930-1960.* New York: Harper and Row, 1968.

O'Neill, John. See Books (No. 153).

Spiegelberg, Herbert. See EXISTENTIALISM (No. 1054).

1349 Strasser, Stephen. "Merleau-Ponty's bijdrage tot de sociaalfilosofie. Interpretatie en critiek." *Tijdschrift voor Filosofie*, vol. XXIX, 1967, pp. 427-470.

Rabil, Albert. See Dissertation and Book (No. 156).

Traub, Essen. See Dissertation (No. 335).

SOUL (see also BODY-SOUL)

1350 Henry, Michel. "Le concept d'âme a-t-il un sens?" *Revue Philosophique de Louvain*, vol. 64, 1966, pp. 5-33. English trans., "Does the concept 'soul' mean anything?" *Philosophy Today*, vol. XIII, 1969, pp. 94-114.

Racette, J. See BODY (No. 968).

SOUND

1351 Smith, F. J. "Vers une phénoménologie du son." *Revue de Métaphysique et de Morale*, vol. 73, 1968, pp. 328-343.

SOVIET UNION

1352 Rossanda, Rossna. "Revolutionary intellectuals and the Soviet Union." *The Socialist Register*, 1973. London: The Merlin Press.

SPACE (see also PERCEPTION)

Hamrick, William S. See Dissertations (No. 291).

Kockelmans, Joseph. See PERCEPTION (Nos. 1251, 1252, and 1253).

SPEECH (see LANGUAGE and COMMUNICATION)

Froman, Wayne. See LANGUAGE (No. 285).

STRUCTURALISM

Boon, James A. See Lévi-Strauss (No. 804).

Charron, Ghyslain. See Nos. 818 and 819.

1353 Cebik, L. B. "*Structuralism*, by Jacques Ehrmann, ed." *Georgia Review*, Vol. XXXVI, no. 2, Summer 1972, pp. 233-237.

1354 Crémant, Roger. *Les Matinées structuralistes*, suivies d'un Discours sur l'écriture et précédées d'une Introduction critique par Albert K+++. Paris: Robert Laffont, 1969.

Culler, Jonathan. See PHENOMENOLOGY (No. 1268).

Daly, James. See PHENOMENOLOGY (No. 1270).

1355   Donato, Eugenio. "The two languages of criticism," pp. 89-97 in Richard Macksey and Eugenio Donato, eds., *The Language of criticism and the Sciences of Man: The Structuralist Controversy*. Baltimore: Johns Hopkins University Press, 1969. (Discussion, pp. 110-124).

1356   Edie, James M. "Was Merleau-Ponty a structuralist?" *Semiotica*, vol. IV, 1971, pp. 297-323.

1357   Garcia Canclini, Nestor. "Merleau-Ponty leido después del estructuralismo," pp. 83-99, in *Temas de Filosofía contemporánea*, Ed. por Emilio Sosa Lopez. Buenos Aires: Editorial Sudamericana, 1971.

1358   Mepham, John. "The structuralist sciences and philosophy," pp. 104-137 in David Robey, ed., *Structuralism: An Introduction*. Oxford: Clarendon Press, 1973.

1359   Smith, Colin. "Merleau-Ponty and structuralism." *Journal of the British Society for Phenomenology*, vol. II, no. 3, Oct. 1971, pp. 46-52.

1360   Viet, J. *Les Méthodes structuralistes dans les sciences sociales*. Paris: Mouton, 1965.

1361   Wahl, François. "La philosophie entre l'avant et l'après du structuralisme," pp. 301-441 in O. Ducrot, T. Todorov, D. Sperber, M. Safouan, F. Wahl, *Qu'est-ce que le structuralisme?* Paris: Editions du Seuil, 1968.

STRUCTURE

Bonomi, Andrea. See Books (No. 210).

1362   Boudon, Raymond. *A quoi sert la notion de 'structure'? Essai sur la notion de structure dans les sciences humaines*. Paris: Gallimard, 1968. English trans. *The Uses of Structure*. London: Heinemann, 1971.

Mbwaki, A. M. See BODY (No. 956).

1363   Panaccio, Claude. "Structure et signification dans l'oeuvre de Merleau-Ponty." *Dialogue*, vol. IX, 1970-1971, pp. 374-380.

SUBJECTIVITY

Bertram, Maryane J. See Dissertations (No. 264).

Sallis, John. See TIME (No. 1373).

SYMBOL

1364 Doubrovsky, J. J. "Existence and symbol." *Philosophy and Phenomenological Research*, vol. XXI, 1960, pp. 229-238.

1365 Xirau, Ramón. "Merleau-Ponty o la encarnación de los simbolos." *Diálogos* (México), no. 6, Sept.-Oct. 1965.

TERROR (see *Humanisme et terreur*)

Bien, Joseph. See Dissertation (No. 266).

THINKING (and thought)

1366 Gauchet, Marcel. "Le lieu de la pensée." *L'Arc*, no. 46, 1971, pp. 19-30.

Gillan, Garth. See BEING (No. 939a).

1367 Yolton, John. *Thinking and Perceiving. A Study in the Philosophy of Mind*. La Salle, Ill.: The Open Court Publishing Co., 1961.

TIME

1368 Bertoldi, Eugene F. "Time in the *Phenomenology of Perception*." *Dialogue*, vol. XIII, no. 4, Dec. 1974, pp. 773-786.

Camele, Anthony M. See HEIDEGGER (No. 778).

1369 Derossi, Giorgio. "Tempo, soggetto, cogito e conoscenza intenzionale diretta (non-mediata) in Merleau-Ponty." *Filosofia* (Torino), vol. XV, 1964, pp. 687-715.

1370 Estrabou, Elma. "La significación del tiempo en la filosofía de Merleau-Ponty." *Revista de Humanides* (Córdoba), vol. II, no. 5, 1962, pp. 58-66.

1371 Florival, Ghislaine. *Le Désir chez Proust. A la recherche du sens*. Louvain-Paris: Nauwelearts, 1971.

Hamrick, William S. See Dissertations (No. 291).

Hunt, Sister Mary Michael. See Dissertations (No. 294).

TIME

1372   Lapointe, François H. "The significance of time in Merleau-Ponty's phenomenology of the body and the world." *The Modern Schoolman*, vol. 49, no. 4, May 1972, pp. 356-366.

Mays, Wolfe. See WHITEHEAD (No. 880).

1373   Sallis, John. "Time, subjectivity and the *Phenomenology of Perception.*" *The Modern Schoolman*, vol. 48, no. 4, May 1971, pp. 343-357.

1374   Spicker, Stuart. "Inner time and lived-through time. Husserl and Merleau-Ponty." *Journal of the British Society for Phenomenology*, vol. IV, no. 3, Oct. 1973, pp. 235-258.

Tilliette, Xavier. See

1375   Waelhens, Alphonse de. "La temporalité," pp. 168-188 in *La Philosophie et les expériences naturelles.* The Hague: Martinus Nijhoff, 1961.

1376   Walton, Roberto J. "Merleau-Ponty y el problema del tiempo." *Cuadernos de Filosofia*, vol. X, Jan.-June 1970, pp. 77-98.

TRUTH

1377   Kwant, Remy C. "Merleau-Ponty's zienswijze omtrent de waarheid." *Handelingen van het XXIIe Vlaams Filologencongress*, 1957, pp. 74-78.

Muglioni, J. See HISTORY (No. 1100).

Paci, Enzo. "Ambiguetà e verità." See AMBIGUITY (No. 916).

Siméon, J.-P. See IDEOLOGIE (No. 1106).

UNCONSCIOUS

1378   Lapointe, Francois H. "Phenomenology, psychoanalysis and the unconscious." *Journal of Phenomenological Psychology*, vol. II, no. 1, Fall 1971, pp. 5-26.

1379   Pontalis, J.-B. "Note sur le problème de l'inconscient chez Merleau-Ponty." *Les Temps Modernes*, 17e année, nos. 184-185, octobre-novembre 1961, pp. 287-303.

VIOLENCE

Langer, Monika M. See Dissertations (No. 302).

Somerville, John. See No. 451.

Walsh, Joseph. See No. 337a.

VISION

Derossi, Giorgio. See ONTOLOGY (No. 549).

Donato, Eugenio. See LANGUAGE (No. 1152).

Funari, E. A. See No. 1274.

Kaufman, Pierre. See No. 539.

Métraux, Alexandre. See No. 1185.

WAR

1380   King, Jonathan. "Philosophy and experience: French intellectuals in the Second World War." *Journal of European Studies*, vol. I, no. 3, Sept. 1971, pp. 198-212.

WORD (see LANGUAGE)

Charlesworth, James H. (See LANGUAGE, No. 1149).

WORLD

Morriston, Charles W. See Dissertation (No. 315).

Touron del Pie, Eliseo. See Books (No. 245).

Toscano, Giuseppe. See No. 1108.

1381   Virasoro, Manuel. "Merleau-Ponty y el mundo al nivel de la percepción." *Ciencia y Fé*, vol. XIII, 1957, pp. 147-155. Trans. by Michael Correa as "Merleau-Ponty and the world of perception." *Philosophy Today*, vol. III, no. 1, Spring 1959, pp. 66-72.

Waelhens, Alphonse de. See REDUCTION (No. 1338).

Wells, Rulon. See OBJECT (No. 1235).

RAYMOND H. FOGLER LIBRARY
DATE DUE